Exile on Wall Street

Exile on Wall Street

One Analyst's Fight to Save the Big Banks from Themselves

Mike Mayo

WILEY

John Wiley & Sons, Inc.

Published by John Wiley & Sons, Inc., Hoboken, New Jersey.
Published simultaneously in Canada.

For general information on our other products and services or for technical support, please
contact our Customer Care Department within the United States at (800) 762-2974,
outside the United States at (317) 572-3993 or fax (317) 572-4002.

Wiley also publishes its books in a variety of electronic formats. Some content that appears
in print may not be available in electronic books. For more information about Wiley
products, visit our web site at www.wiley.com.

Library of Congress Cataloging-in-Publication Data:

ISBN 978-1-118-11546-6; ISBN 978-1-118-20364-4 (ebk);
ISBN 978-1-118-20365-1 (ebk); ISBN 978-1-118-20366-8 (ebk)

Printed in the United States of America
10 9 8 7 6 5 4

Contents

Introduction

Watering Down the Wine

I had an epiphany not long ago. It took place during a dinner conversation at a massive investors' conference in Hong Kong. Over the course of five days, some 1,300 investors showed up, along with another 500 top corporate executives. The former president of Pakistan, Pervez Musharraf, spoke about his country's role in the global economy. Historian Simon Schama discussed the United States' current position in the world, and film director Francis Ford Coppola flew in to talk about the importance of narrative. Asia's economy was sizzling, with a growth rate three times than that of the United States, creating a billion more middle-class citizens—and this event was at the epicenter of that growth. Evidence as to why China would likely overtake the United States as the largest economy within a decade was on full display. Perhaps this was why my daughter was being offered the chance to learn Mandarin in her New York City school.

But what really stood out for me was something someone said over dinner on the first night I arrived. I had just come off a sixteen-hour flight from New York to Hong Kong, one of the longest nonstop flights in the world, and was dining with about a dozen bank analysts from major Asian countries. We were at the Dynasty restaurant, which has a Michelin star and spectacular views of Victoria Harbour, though I was too jet-lagged to appreciate the scenery.

Over the ten-course meal, we went around the table and discussed the current prospects for banks in our specific markets. This was the real point of the meal—to share information—and in this way, we were acting as unofficial ambassadors for our home countries.

The Japanese bank analyst talked about how that government's policies had allowed banks to continue lending to corporate borrowers even though those companies, and many of the banks themselves, should have folded years ago. They were zombies, the walking dead. The Chinese analyst talked about how his country still had tremendous room for growth. Consumer credit in China, as a percentage of the overall economy, was only about one-fifth the level in the United States. The ride would be bumpy for investors in Chinese bank stocks, but the long-term prospects were very promising. Next, the bank analyst from Korea spoke, then Thailand, Indonesia, and so on.

I knew my turn was approaching, and I started thinking about what I would say. At the time, I was in the middle of a very public dispute with Citigroup over some of its accounting practices. Citi didn't like what I had been saying and had adopted a shoot-the-messenger approach. For the past several months, I had been airing my concerns in the media, through outlets like CNBC and the *Wall Street Journal*, and the company either ignored the issues I raised or sniped back at me in the press. It would all come to a head a few weeks after that conference, but in the meantime, the financial community had been following it closely.

This kind of fight was not new to me. I've worked as a bank analyst for the past twenty years, where my job is to study publicly traded financial firms and decide which ones would make the best investments. My research goes out to institutional investors: mutual fund companies, university endowments, public-employee retirement funds, hedge funds, private pensions, and other organizations with large amounts of money. Some individuals I meet with manage $10 billion or more, which they invest in banks and other stocks. If they believe what I say, they invest accordingly, trading through my firm.

Here's the difficult part, though. For about half of my career, especially the last five years or so, most big banks hadn't been good investments. They'd been *terrible* investments, down 50, 60, 70 percent or more. In fact, if you didn't even do any analysis and just assumed the worst about bank stocks—that is, that they weren't good places to invest your money, that they weren't well-run companies—you'd have done OK lately. Not much analysis required.

Over the years, I've been saying this loudly and repeatedly. As far back as 1999, I pointed out certain problems in the banking sector—things like excessive risks, outsized compensation for bankers, more aggressive lending. Those same problems would build throughout the 2000s and ultimately erupt during the financial crisis of 2007–2008, taking down Lehman Brothers, Bear Stearns, and dozens of smaller banks and thrifts. However, taking a negative position doesn't win you many friends in the banking sector. I've been yelled at, conspicuously ignored, threatened with legal action, and mocked by executives at the companies I've covered, all with the intent of persuading me to soften my stance.

The response from some places where I've worked has not been much better—I've seen the banks from all sides, not only as an analyst covering them but also as an employee working for them. At times, colleagues were trying to drum up business from the same banks that I was critiquing, and when I said things they didn't like, I faced a backlash. I've bet my career on my convictions, and at times that stance has forced me to find a new job—and has even led to my being fired.

Almost every step of my career has been a struggle. When I first tried to get a job on Wall Street, I applied to two dozen firms over five years before landing my first interview. Since then I've worked at UBS, Lehman, Credit Suisse, Prudential Securities, and Deutsche Bank, among others.

Yet my experience has been worth the struggle. I'm still in the game and I still love my work. I was the only Wall Street analyst to testify to the Senate Banking Committee in 2002 about conflicts of interest on Wall Street, even as other analysts were sanctioned for pumping up tech stocks and not spotting debacles like Enron—at the time, the biggest bankruptcy in history. In 2010, I again testified, this time for the commission investigating the causes of the recent financial crisis. In part, that invitation came because I was named by *Fortune* magazine as one of eight people who saw the crisis coming. Over the decade leading up to the crisis, I produced about 10,000 pages of cautionary research on the banking sector.

I fundamentally believe in the U.S. banking system. It's the best in the world, and throughout our history, it's done the most good for the most people. Our banks are excellent at their primary function of allocating capital to the most promising opportunities, which leads to the creation and expansion of companies, innovative products, better job prospects, and an overall increase in the standard of living. Because the U.S. economic system allows individuals to be rewarded on merit, people are motivated to work harder, move to new locations with better employment prospects, take risks, and retrain when they have a shot within a fair system.

Look at the results: Even with the recent crisis, we have the world's largest economy, leading worker productivity and mobility, more innovation in fast-growing sectors like technology and health care, and the world's top universities. Over the past generation, the number of people worldwide living in a capitalist society has more than tripled. When it comes to exports, France has wine; we have capitalism.

■ ■ ■

So at the dinner conversation that Sunday night in Hong Kong, when my turn came to speak, I talked about how the U.S. banking sector was still climbing out of the holes it had dug for itself during the financial crisis.

"Our banks have repaired their balance sheets, with a reduction in problem loans and new capital," I said. "So the safety of the system is better, and that's good. The issue is one of 'all dressed up and nowhere to go.' That is, the chance of big failures has dramatically declined, so the U.S. banks look better, but I'm not sure where the banks will get their growth."

Another analyst asked me to clarify.

"U.S. banks are a lighter version of what's taken place in Japan," I said. "We're in year two of what has been a twenty-year cycle in Japan. I'm not saying that it'll take U.S. banks and the economy that long to fully recover, but the real question is how much longer—one, three, five years—will it take to get back to normal. That's the question. There are still big headwinds."

"What about Citi?" one of the other analysts interrupted me. "It's a dog, right, Mike?"

I hesitated. Citigroup encapsulated all of my views on the current problems of the banking sector—the wasted potential, the fact that so few at the company seemed embarrassed or upset with its performance, the way that many of its problems were reconstituted versions of the problems that had plagued it over the past two decades: excess risk, aggressive accounting, and outsized compensation, among others.

Before I could formulate a diplomatic answer, one of the other analysts spoke up, and this is what would linger in my mind. "All U.S. banks are like that," he said with a laugh.

I froze, feeling myself growing defensive. It was a little like the situation where you're allowed to criticize people in your own family but instantly defend them as soon as anyone else does. My reflexive answer was that all U.S. banks *aren't* like that. There are hundreds of smaller regional banks that had little to do with the financial crisis and even a few large banks that performed better than the rest. But you don't hear much about them, because on the whole the bad operators have been bad enough to overshadow the good, and they've helped foster a poor reputation for U.S. banks, a kind of negative brand for our financial system. It's as if the French had decided to water down their wine before shipping it out.

In fact, the root causes of the crisis are still in place. Large banks have enough clout to beat the living daylights out of anybody who gets in the way—politicians, the press, or analysts like me. They can effectively send you into exile, and they get their way more often than not. Look no further than CEO compensation. I have no problem with individuals getting paid a lot of money if they deliver sustainable results. Yet bank CEO pay has already climbed back near precrisis levels, even though twelve of the thirteen largest U.S. banks would have failed if not for government intervention. The CEOs of two banks, SunTrust and KeyCorp, each made more than $20 million over the period from 2008 through 2010, even while their companies lost hundreds of millions of dollars. That's not capitalism; that's entitlement.

Here's a starkly contrasting scenario: In the middle of the Japanese financial crisis in the late 1990s, the CEO of one of Japan's big four investment firms—Yamaichi Securities—appeared on television to apologize for the actions of his company, and he broke down in tears. That's unusual for any executive, but especially by the reserved cultural standards of Japan. I don't need to see tears from the executives of U.S. banks, but at least some recognition that the real owners of these companies—the shareholders—matter.

Bloomberg Businessweek ran a March 2011 profile of the chairman of Citigroup, Dick Parsons, which included some quotes about the events of the financial crisis. As Parsons described it, "Timmy Geithner would say, 'Call me directly because this is too important an institution to go down.'" You read that right: Parsons called the Secretary of the Treasury "Timmy" in an interview, which does not exactly acknowledge the authority of the Secretary, a post once occupied by Alexander Hamilton. He also talked about why the government had to bail Citi out, by describing the likely consequences if the company had been allowed to go under: "You wouldn't be able to buy a loaf of bread or clear a check," Parsons said. "It would be like Egypt. People would be out on the streets." Can that really be true? Citigroup's continued existence is the only thing separating the United States and Egypt? What comes across in the profile is a sense of arrogance and insider access. It was the equivalent of flipping the bird at shareholders, the Treasury, and the country at the same time.

I get frustrated with banks—I get furious at times—because they should hold themselves to a higher standard. Irresponsible actions by these institutions have put our economy and our entire capitalist system at risk, and the rest of the world has noticed. In August 2011, the Russian prime minister, Vladimir Putin, said that the United States is "living like parasites" off the global economy. This statement felt like a particularly stinging rebuke to me, since both of my grandfathers escaped a socially and economically unjust Russia and made tremendous sacrifices to create a successful life for my family in the United States. I have a kinship to that legacy to ensure a better world for my three children—it's literally in my blood. But I also have an urgent worry that the successes of the past generations are beginning to run out of steam, in part because of systemic problems in our financial sector. Banks are integral to how our system functions. We can and should do better.

That means bank executives, particularly CEOs, need to operate as stewards of something larger than themselves and not just grab the fast buck and run. Bankers, like all people, respond to incentives, and these days the incentives on Wall Street are set up to reward short-term behavior. It's simply too easy to jump in and grab all the money you can rather than adopting a broader view that considers whether certain deals or mergers or trades are in the long-term interest of the firm or the country.

As I write this in the late summer of 2011, the market is showing volatility that would have been extreme before the financial crisis but now is more a permanent part of the market. Investor sentiment seems to change from unusually positive to forcefully negative in a matter of days. This stems from a fundamental lack of trust and confidence in the financial system, and how can it not?

Even after the shortcomings exposed during the crisis, banks still show aggressive accounting and opaque disclosures. Even after CEOs of failed companies walked away with eight-figure paychecks, compensation is still rigged in favor of senior management. Even after big banks used their power to get rules changed that helped their companies—or, really, their senior managers (after all, most of the rank and file at banks are more like Main Street than Wall Street)—the companies use their power to block actions that would allow for better checks and balances. Lumped together, all of these actions lead you to wonder: "How did they get away with it? And how is it still happening?"

This is not a book solely about the latest financial crisis. Instead, it is about the larger historical arc of the banking industry and how I have spent my career trying to warn investors and banks about the problems I've seen. Most of the behaviors that caused the crisis were in place long before the downturn, and—even worse—most have not changed since then. Some people want to look at the crisis as an isolated event, a single discrete occurrence that can be sealed off and looked back on in the past tense. But that's not accurate. The crisis didn't occur because of something that banks *did*. No, it was the natural consequence of the way banks *are*, even today.

That was my epiphany—the analyst in Hong Kong was dead right. Not all U.S. banks are poor operators, but as a group, the biggest ones are. Because of this ongoing pattern of bad behavior, we're tainting an important global export of this country—capitalism—and showing that while it has the potential to raise people's standard of living and reallocate capital more effectively than any other economic system, it also has a lot of room for improvement. We are watering down the wine.

Chapter 1

"God's Work" at the Fed

Unlike a lot of people on Wall Street, I have no pedigree. No Ivy League degree, no prep schools, no internships arranged by a well-placed uncle. In fact, my whole family is a collection of immigrants and outsiders. On my father's side, my great-grandfather came from Odessa, Russia. In 1905, during the pogroms in that city, his brother was killed by a Cossack guard. My great-grandfather ended up strangling the guard before sneaking out of the country. He arrived in the United States at age thirty-seven, and his last name, Koretzky, was cut down to Kerr. A year later, he was able to arrange for several other family members to get out of Russia, as well, including his son, my grandfather. They entered the United States through Ellis Island in 1906, and for a while the family was so poor that the oldest son had to leave school at age twelve to sell flypaper on the street corners of South Philly.

My mom was raised in an Orthodox Jewish immigrant family in Baltimore, with very traditional values. Her father emigrated from Gomel, then part of Russia, in 1907, also via Ellis Island. Her mother died of cancer when she was just three, and she grew up in her aunt's house. My mom was an original thinker, into sushi and yoga before either one became fashionable. I often came home to find her upside down, doing a headstand in a corner of the house. My parents split up when I was three years old, and although most people in her family never left the Baltimore area, she settled in Washington, DC. It's only forty miles away, but it might as well have been a different planet to her family. She worked at the local TV station to support her life as a single mom with three kids. She remarried when I was five, in 1968, to the person she considered her soul mate. My mother and stepdad met at a bridge tournament where they discovered that they both enjoyed the same brand of cheap Scotch.

My stepdad—who raised me along with my mom—also immigrated to the United States, and his story is also that of an outsider. He grew up in Romania in the 1930s, and during his childhood, he watched his country go from a Romanian monarchy, to dysfunctional democracy, to dictatorship, to a Nazi takeover, and then to Communist rule after World War II. When he was seventeen, my stepdad tried to escape from the country, because of violent threats against Romanian Jews.

His goal was to get to Palestine, which was then controlled by the British. He had the equivalent of $350, money he had made by selling cigarettes, gum, and candy on the black market. His first escape attempt failed—he made it across the border to Hungary but was captured by the secret police and sent back to Romania. On his second attempt, he was again caught. On the third attempt, as with my great-grandfather, he had to kill someone in self-defense (in this case, a Romanian guard) in order to finally make it out.

In 1948, he went to Palestine to fight for the Jews' new homeland. When I was a child, I remember him telling me that he would gladly have given his life if he knew it would have resulted in a Jewish state. That willingness to trade personal sacrifice for patriotic goals really resonated with me. It wasn't just about getting ahead and taking care of yourself—there were larger principles at work.

Not that this got in the way of his willingness to hustle a little bit. He was street smart and spoke eight languages, in part from his dealings on the black market. For a while, he smuggled watches across the border from Switzerland into Italy. When he later wrote a memoir of this time in his life, he remembered having hundreds of them strapped to his body under his clothes, so many that he ticked like a time bomb.

He served in the Israeli navy and later the merchant marine, and he got into the United States by jumping ship in Florida, later becoming a citizen. By the mid-1960s, he landed in the Washington, DC, area, where he started and ran an aluminum-siding business. He had changed his last name after his escape from Romania; at the time of his move to Florida, he was known as "May'ami," which was an anglicized version of the Hebrew phrase "to my nation." In Florida, people called him "Mike Miami," so he changed his name to Mayo. When I was growing up, every year on the first day of school I had to explain that the last name that I used wasn't Kerr but Mayo.

My stepdad told me constantly as a kid that World War III with Russia was an absolute certainty. He slept with a handgun by his bed his entire life. I would wake up to hear him screaming profanities at his sales rep, every curse word in the book, demanding that the rep bring in more leads. I was astonished one day to find out that this salesperson was a woman, Vickie, who was good at her job and continued to work for my stepdad for years despite the daily shouting matches.

When he opened a Romanian restaurant with my mother in 1981 called the Vagabond in Bethesda, Maryland, he was comfortable speaking Spanish to the busboys and English to the customers and could hold his own in political discussions with the diplomats who came in. As my mom put it to a restaurant reviewer once, "He can speak, read, sing, and cook fluently in eight languages." My stepdad did all the cooking at this restaurant, including recipes his mother used to make, and the place once won "Best Duck" in the restaurant section of *Washingtonian Magazine*. He loved vodka and cigars, and, really, he just loved life. He used to say that he didn't want to wait to be an *alter kocker*, which is Yiddish and translates roughly to "old fart," before he could enjoy himself. Once when he was traveling in France, some people said to him in French—thinking that he couldn't understand—that his giant cigar looked like a prick. "Yes," he shot back in perfect French, "but it doesn't taste like one."

■ ■ ■

When it came time for me to pick a college, I went with the University of Maryland for my bachelor's degree, because the couple of people in my family who had attended college went there. Later I got an MBA at George Washington University at night while working full time. Both schools were good experiences—Maryland's math department was in the top twenty in the country when I was there; GWU had a respectable business program—but neither one makes the doors fly open on Wall Street.

I know this because my early attempts to get a job there fell flat. I still have the rejection letters, every one of them. Prudential: "We have considered your background and, although it is impressive, we find that our current staffing requirements are not consistent with your objectives and abilities." Goldman Sachs: "If we do not contact you directly, you can assume that there are no appropriate openings available." I like looking through this folder of initial rejections, because some of the firms in there don't exist anymore—Drexel Burnham, Kidder Peabody, Bankers Trust. But at the time I was crushed. I didn't get one interview.

During this time, I was working at IBM, where I stayed for only a few years, just long enough to realize that a corporate culture like that wasn't for me. I remember the old-timers wearing lapel pins that showed the number of years they'd been at the company—twenty-five years, thirty years. My friends and I would keep our IBM ID tags on when we went to the bars at night, thinking (incorrectly) that they would impress the ladies.

As the Wall Street rejections continued to pile up, I took a job at the Federal Reserve in Washington, DC, where I first learned to analyze bank deals. The salary represented a pay cut from IBM. I'd be a "GSer," referring to the government service pay scale, something that everyone in my family had always regarded suspiciously, given their natural mistrust of bureaucrats. I tried explaining that staffers at the Fed aren't technically in the GS system, but that didn't cut it. Still, I wouldn't trade my time there for anything. It was at the Fed that my thoughts on the banking industry took shape and where I learned about the crucial role that objective analysis plays as a check and balance on the sector.

I worked there in the late 1980s and early 1990s. Alan Greenspan was the Fed chairman, but this was before he became a cult figure in the financial markets, and at the time his predecessor, Paul Volcker, had left a lasting impression at the agency. To this day, Paul Volcker is my hero—the six-foot-seven iconoclast who was willing to raise interest rates in the early 1980s in order to stop inflation. That measure led to a necessary but painful slowdown in the economy, with temporarily higher unemployment and interest rates as high as 20 percent. It drew fierce protests—farmers drove their tractors in front of the Fed's head-quarters in the Eccles building on C Street in Washington, and one congressman wanted Volcker impeached—but it successfully ended the stagflation of the prior decade. Volcker was willing to take hard, necessary steps, a rarity for many public figures at that level. When his term ended in 1987, President Reagan would replace him and bring in Greenspan.

Since the financial crisis, history has come back to Volcker. Greenspan's legacy became tarnished by the 1998 bailout of hedge fund Long-Term Capital Management, which represented a shift in the Fed's strategy. It signaled to the market that if conditions got bad enough, the Fed would step in to save floundering banks. This strategy carried through to the Internet bubble and post-Greenspan to the crisis in 2007 and 2008, when unusual policy actions protected the banks and others from their own mistakes.

After the latest financial crisis and the real estate debacle, Volcker looks increasingly correct about the need for effective regulation. I respect him most because he never bought into the line—invariably offered by bankers—that regulators should do what's best for the banks because that will do the most good for the country.

Volcker always took the opposite approach: The goal of the Federal Reserve, and of all outsiders with any kind of oversight role on the financial system, isn't just to help the banking industry. It's not to strip away any regulation or constraint and turn Wall Street into a casino. Instead, it's to ensure that the banking industry remains stable and helps our economy thrive. Volcker was an outsider, and he argued for a big, bold line between the public sector and the private sector that it regu-lates. Investor and philanthropist George Soros, a friend of Volcker's, once called him "the exemplary public servant—he embodies that old idea of civic virtue."

That was his legacy at the Fed when I was there, and we believed that. Civic virtue. Detachment from the companies we were overseeing.

Lloyd Blankfein, the CEO of Goldman Sachs, said in a notorious 2009 interview that he thought the firm was doing "God's work," and he was promptly ripped to shreds in the press for it. But during my time at the Fed, we genuinely believed that we were performing a valuable public service: protecting the banking system for the benefit of our country. We weren't getting rich—administrative assistants on Wall Street at the time made more than the average Fed employee—but we were performing a crucial function in the economy and helping the country advance. This was partly a reflection of the times. It was the tail end of the Cold War, when, after all my stepdad's warnings, World War III had never happened. America had won, and we proved that capitalism was the better economic system. America had a meritocracy that allowed people to rise up through their own talents and efforts. And by harnessing that desire, capitalism could do amazing things. It could direct money to the most productive avenues in order to create wealth and raise living standards. It could transform nations and defeat tyrants. But it needed some checks and balances to function optimally.

■ ■ ■

My first few months at the Fed were like Marine Corps boot camp. I was part of a class of two dozen wide-eyed junior regulators, meeting daily in a classroom in nearby Foggy Bottom. I learned to write reports that made a clear argument for whether a deal should be approved or not. Don't hedge, don't waste anyone's time. Clarify your argument and substantiate it. In our early training, we got lectures from FBI investigators about fraud—I remember one story about what it was like to nab embezzlers or people running other long-term scams. When you finally arrest them, the FBI investigator told us, they're almost relieved. "It's like pulling a knife out of their back," he said. Another finance expert talked to us about the typical growth rate of banks and how some exceptionally rapid growth in the industry shouldn't be celebrated but questioned. "If something grows like a weed, maybe it is a weed," he said. That quote would come back to me when I watched home loans at big banks grow through the roof from the late 1990s to the late 2000s.

More than anything, we were grounded in the basics of bank finance, specifically bank financial statements, which show items differently than the rest of the corporate world. Money is the product that banks sell—loans, deposits, and securities—as opposed to goods and services. Instead of millions of iPods in inventory, you see millions of loans to companies and individuals. In other industries, loans are typically liabilities because as a borrower you're on the hook to pay that money back. But banks are lenders, meaning that loans are assets. The more loans a bank makes—assuming it has done its homework and reasonably believes that the loans went to reliable, upstanding people who are going to pay them back—the better off that bank is.

As complicated as high-level finance has become in the past decade, at its core, banking is a simple business. Bankers borrow money at a certain interest rate, mostly as customer deposits, then lend it out at a higher rate, and they get to keep the difference. For a long time banks operated on the 3-6-3 rule: Borrow at 3 percent, lend at 6 percent, and be on the golf course by 3 P.M. From the 1940s through the late 1960s, this was the guiding principle. Banks were closer to utilities—very reliable and without big boom-and-bust scenarios. There were some laws in place, like Glass-Steagall, which came about after the 1929 crash and prevented consumer banks and investment banks from being owned and operated by the same company. This ensured that traditional banks, which took relatively limited amounts of risk with customer deposits by making loans, were separate from investment banks, which were using their own capital to take greater risks. Those rules were like governors on a car engine—they helped prevent banks from growing too fast, and they kept the overall industry reasonably safe. They also limited bank returns, which is why bankers wanted them overturned.

When I arrived at the Fed, the country had just gone through the savings and loan (S&L) crisis of the late 1980s—the first financial problem I understood as an adult, though it wouldn't be the last. In fact, it shows how many banking crises boil down to the same fundamental problems. S&Ls, also known as thrifts, are a narrower form of traditional banks that mostly take deposits from individuals and make loans for people to buy homes. The crisis happened because small local thrifts got too big, too fast, by expanding outside these core areas. The S&L

failures cost the taxpayers since their deposits were insured like ordinary bank deposits, meaning that the government paid back depositors when the S&Ls couldn't.

Ineffective changes in regulation were at the heart of the problem. Thrifts, which were not under direct Fed supervision, were always less regulated than conventional banks, and the rules became even more lax after Congress passed several pieces of legislation in the early 1980s. These greatly expanded the types of loans that thrifts could make and the interest rates they could pay depositors above prior tight interest rate ceilings. If a bank or thrift wanted more deposits, it could offer more interest and watch the deposits flow in. This is exactly what happened, but the deposits were of the volatile type, "hot money," because these deposits tend to chase the highest rates and can't be relied on in tough times.

Similarly, banks can always make more loans if they find less stable borrowers or offer unusually attractive terms. In this case, S&Ls made more loans for risky construction projects, things like fast-food franchises, wind farms, and casinos. The safer loans of the time, residential mortgages, declined from 80 percent of the total in 1982 to 56 percent by 1986, and banks replaced them with riskier loans funded by hot-money deposits. Over the next four years, from 1982 to 1986, the thrift industry posted ridiculous growth, with loans and other assets doubling to $1.2 billion, a potential recipe for disaster.

For a while, real estate boomed, and everyone in banking—not just the thrifts—wanted a piece of that growth. The economy was humming. Demand for office space went up, rents were pushed higher, construction flourished, and banks actively looked for builders that they could lend to, creating a virtuous cycle. Yet expansion like that isn't sustainable, because it's driven by an excess supply of financing that outpaced the underlying growth in the economy and population. By the late 1980s, as it became clear that actual demand for office space was much lower than supply, real estate developers started having problems paying back the loans. When credit started to turn bad, thrifts and many banks were unprepared for the losses. The problems started in the United States and then spread around the world. (If this all sounds familiar, it should.) About 1,000 S&Ls went out of business, and the final cost of the crisis was $160 billion, including $132 billion from federal taxpayers. From that point on, the mistakes the banks and thrifts made were variations of the same theme—some combination of regulatory changes and overheated growth—and would have even bigger consequences.

The S&L crisis was the dark side of capitalism, and it showed that without some checks and balances on the system, the potential for excesses could weaken it from within. Capital could be misdirected—frittered away or destroyed—and not only would an opportunity be lost, but people's lives would be devastated. That was our function at the Fed: to monitor the financial system and prevent similar catastrophes from happening again. We didn't have the money of Wall Street, but we had power.

This balance was the subject of discussions that my friend and Fed colleague Hank and I used to have during our early-morning runs. Making our way down Constitution Avenue to the Lincoln Memorial, we would debate who was more powerful: Fed chairman Alan Greenspan or Citicorp CEO John Reed. I would stress that the Fed chairman held more power, since his control of monetary policy would determine the strength of the economy and could even swing national elections. As we ran up the steps of the Lincoln Memorial to touch the wall and then back down again, Hank would say that John Reed could move billions of dollars with a phone call and do so without all of the second-guessing by government underlings.

Around the Reflecting Pool we would press on, past the Jefferson Memorial. I told him that I had once seen a fax in the office that laid out the money Citicorp needed to raise to meet the government's capital requirements. "See?" I said. "Greenspan calls the shots for John Reed!" Hank huffed something about the strength of the CEO during periods when banks were healthier as we slowed to a jog in front of the Grecian columns of the Fed headquarters at the Eccles building, one of Washington's Beaux Arts landmarks. Little did I know that this concept—the relative clout between regulators and the private sector—would continue to play out for the next two decades, particularly in periods of crisis.

■ ■ ■

During my time at the Fed, I worked in the merger-approval division or, as we answered the phone, "Applications." Two banks that wanted to merge had to get clearance from the Fed. Usually that happened at one of the twelve Fed regional banks around the country, but if there were any unusual circumstances—for example, if one of the banks was foreign owned, or particularly large—it would be handled in Washington.

I looked at hundreds of deals in my time there. In one twelve-month period, I analyzed 119 deals. If we thought a merger might be more risky than we were comfortable with, we would go back to the bank and say that management had to make some changes to the deal terms. Often the banks had to set aside more capital—meaning they needed a bigger fund of reserves in case something should go wrong down the road. As we saw it, we were defending the country, in a way. As the banking industry became more integrated, we were establishing international capital standards, and this was going to make the system safer. In the end, it would be just a little bit better for everybody.

The Fed had extremely high standards, so every report had to be perfect, down to the last word and statistic. Literally, my boss would read my reports and move the word "however" to another part of the sentence, perhaps simply to send a signal to me about the scrutiny of our work. The logic needed to be perfect, too, laid out as concisely as possible so as not to waste the time of anybody reading it and also to uphold legal scrutiny in the unlikely but still possible scenario that the Fed was sued over one of these decisions. It was as if I were required to write an A+ paper every time.

Most of my work would be reviewed by my bosses and then filed away with a stamp TO RECORDS, where it was likely never read again. I imagined the warehouse scene at the end of *Raiders of the Lost Ark*, with crates of old reports piled to the ceiling. I was one of about ten people in DC reviewing merger applications, and the job involved some tedium and little visibility. I was conscious that we didn't have many resources. There's a daily trade newspaper in the industry, called *American Banker*, and because it's expensive, we weren't allowed to get individual subscriptions at the Fed. Instead, a single copy would get circulated around, with a distribution list ranking names in order of seniority. By the time it got to me, it was three and a half weeks old.

But the money, or lack of it, was less important than working with those who had responsibility, authority, and power—the people who set policy for the national economy. We ate breakfast in the Fed cafeteria, with wall-to-wall windows looking toward Constitution Avenue, one block south, and to the monuments of the Mall beyond. In the distance were the Washington Monument and the Lincoln Memorial, symbols that inspired and reminded us about the importance of the work we were doing. A regular group of people met for breakfast most mornings. I used to run to work from my apartment in the Adams Morgan neighborhood of Washington, where I had pinned up a photo of Alan Greenspan torn from a cover story about him in *The Economist* magazine. I often left home early so that I'd have time to use the gym at the Fed and then get a giant plate of eggs and pancakes, smothered in butter and syrup. (I ate terribly in those days.)

There was a strong sense that we were on the outside and that this was a healthy separation of bankers from federal agencies. I remember one of the mornings after the investment bank Drexel Burnham failed in 1990. People at the breakfast table talked about how the lights had been on late in the building the night before and how pizzas had been delivered. Drexel had been running commercials about how it helped communities—part of a campaign to polish its image—and I made a joke about how I wondered whether it was now part of the United Way. Maybe I could donate to the fund, I said, drawing some laughs. We talked about how some people involved in that fiasco must have lost a lot of money, but the people at that table knew nobody on Wall Street. We were like the cops patrolling outside an upscale party at the Plaza. It doesn't matter how the party ends—the lives of the people standing outside the doors aren't going to change much.

Some mornings, a few of the Fed's power players would join us. Bill Taylor came by many days. He was the senior regulator, overseeing major financial crises—one of his biggest was the shutdown of the Bank of Credit and Commerce International—and he reported directly to Greenspan. When Greenspan testified before Congress, Taylor was the person behind him, whispering into his ear. On the mornings when Taylor sat down to eat breakfast with us, the table practically trembled. I remember a conversation in which one of Taylor's junior staff came to him at the breakfast table and asked about a pending bank deal. "Tell them to raise more capital or the answer is no," Taylor said, then turned back to his coffee. We felt like we were batboys in the dugout at Yankee stadium.

Bill Taylor was a culture carrier for the institution, and he had very high standards. Once, when a snowstorm was headed toward DC and most of the government was expecting a day off, Taylor said that the people at our department would all be at work the next day no matter what. Someone asked him why. "Because we're not wimps," he said.

He also set the tone for the Fed as a whole, favoring straightforward logic over nuance. In another discussion, when somebody in Congress suggested relaxing the size of loans that a bank could make from 15 percent to 25 percent of its total size, there was a big theoretical debate among various PhDs and staffers, until Taylor entered and gave the rationale for opposing this move: "Because then it could only take four loans to make a bank fail whereas now it takes seven." In other words, there was a presumption that banks would push the boundaries and get into trouble, a perennial race to the bottom in terms of standards, and so they needed rules to prevent them from doing so. End of debate.

From humble roots as a Chicago bank examiner, Taylor rose to lead all the examiners, and relayed his confidence to those under him. He instilled a spirit of purpose to our job. In a Fed publication in 1990, he said, "We have been able to challenge the people and they have responded magnificently. They sense it as their duty. They are prepared to make sacrifices and most importantly have a tremendous desire and ability to perform. They are the force. I would take them anywhere." How could you not want to give your all for a leader like that?

■ ■ ■

I made it into the Fed's main conference room on exactly two occasions, when one of my cases, a bank in Kansas called Cedar Vale, had a broader issue that required that my work be reviewed, discussed, and voted on by the Board of Governors of the Fed, which included the Fed chairman and six other governors. This meant that I would be at the board table with none other than Alan Greenspan himself. I was one year into the job.

To this point, I'd had little interaction with the top people. Once, when I had reserved the Fed's tennis court after work, I arrived to find Alan Greenspan still playing with one of the Fed governors, a man named Wayne Angell. They had the slot immediately before me, and Greenspan asked if he could stay to finish his match. I wanted to say, "Only if you tell me what you're going to do with interest rates," but instead I simply nodded politely. Another time, a year or so later, I would see him at a backyard barbecue hosted by Taylor. Greenspan arrived wearing long checkered slacks, and his guest was Barbara Walters. Later, near the end of my time at the Fed, I called his office to ask for a photo of myself with him. He obliged with an autographed photo inscribed "Good luck, Mike, Best Wishes. Regards, Alan Greenspan." My joke later on would be that the chairman had the same picture in his office, with my best wishes.

But the board meeting would be the first time I had any professional contact with people of this caliber. I was told that the discussion about Cedar Vale could take any direction. The seven governors, including Greenspan, would take a vote on whether to approve the merger or not. They might ask me questions. They might not. They may use the results of the Cedar Vale bank case to set policy for the rest of the 12,000 banks we regulated. Or not. They could ask about the meaning of a word in a sentence, or even highlight a typo.

With two days' notice, we found out that "it was time." I got ready, meticulously preparing my notes and selecting my best dark blue suit to get pressed. I got a haircut and shined my shoes. If nothing else, I was going to look good. On the day of the meeting, instead of entering the boardroom directly, I waited along with my managers in the anteroom while the board discussed other business. Prior to this, my biggest presentation was when I had helped get a friend elected as an officer in my college fraternity by giving a speech complete with charts and graphs.

After a few minutes, the secretary of the board—and a regular at the breakfast table—said, "Now, the Cedar Vale case." My boss showed me my chair, and he sat next to me, both of us at the foot of the long, rectangular table. The space where the Fed governors meet is awe-inspiring. It looks like God's conference room. The ceiling is two stories high, with a massive chandelier in the middle, suspended over a twenty-seven-foot conference table made of Honduran mahogany. Despite a couple of renovations, the room still holds the original design of the architect who created the Eccles building, back in the 1930s. During World War II, a couple of key strategy meetings between the United

States and the British were held here, as it was one of the most secure sites in Washington. These days, the Fed conference room is where the Federal Open Market Committee meets to set interest rates.

All of my senior managers were seated on the right side, including Bill Taylor in the middle, and the lawyers on the left. The Fed governors were split on both sides at the far end, and Chairman Greenspan was at the head. I was ready with numbers about ratios, trends, totals, and details of the merger proposal. The main issue under debate was whether Cedar Vale met the Fed's guidelines to buy another bank and whether it was using too much debt for the purchase. The discussion went back and forth, with a few governors asking different questions. In prior months on other proposals, some of my analyst colleagues said that they had answered a couple of questions during their own ordeals. In my case, I would like to think that I could have made a difference. I would also like to think that I could have even answered a question. Yet I simply sat there for six terrifying minutes without saying a word.

At one point, the tennis-playing governor, Wayne Angell, spoke up about applying big bank guidelines to this much smaller bank in Kansas, which had the potential to increase the likelihood that the deal would be approved. The room was quiet for a moment. I was specifically asked about how a big bank ratio applied to this smaller bank, and I had no idea of the answer—with the secretary, six Fed governors, and Chairman Greenspan himself looking to me for the answer.

Taylor spoke up and saved me. "Why is this necessary?" he asked. There was a bit more back-and-forth, and finally Chairman Greenspan decided they would take up the discussion in a future board meeting. That meant another report that I had to prepare with a senior colleague and a very thorough background check to make sure that Angell had no ties to the Cedar Vale bank in the past. He was born and educated in Kansas; his dissertation was titled "The History of Commercial Banking in Kansas." I was told to search through all the documents related to this case, going back years and years, from a range of sources, for any mention of Governor Angell. In other words, was he so close to the situation that he should recuse himself? We found no evidence, but I certainly did check.

At the next meeting a few weeks later—same seating arrangement with me at the far end of the table from Chairman Greenspan, same nerves, same intense preparation, both professional and regarding personal grooming—Angell conceded. Taylor's regulatory position held firm. Cedar Vale bank would have to do more to get its merger approved by the Fed (though ultimately it was denied). On the way back to our offices, Taylor's only words to me were "Much ado about nothing" as he strode briskly to his next task.

■ ■ ■

To me, these individuals were the equivalent of Plato's fictitious Men of Silver, soldiers of the public interest who looked not for money or fame but only to serve. My perception of their sense of duty, however, would soften in time, especially years later. Ernie Patrikis, longtime chief counsel and a thirty-year veteran at the New York Fed, took a job at the insurance giant AIG in 1999, where his salary presumably increased by an order of magnitude. He was at that company for eight years, part of which he spent trying to help AIG deal with its massive regulatory problems.

The head of the New York Fed took a job at the big investment bank Goldman Sachs and later had a well-publicized affair with the head of the Boston Fed. The New York position is incredibly powerful—that bank does not report directly to DC, so the person who runs that is generally considered the second most powerful in the agency, behind only the chairman. As for Angell, the governor who raised issues during my Cedar Vale case, he eventually quit to take a job at investment bank Bear Stearns. He began making predictions about the direction of interest rates just months after leaving the Fed, and his initial calls were so accurate that they raised eyebrows and triggered an investigation about possible leaked information. (The investigation turned up no wrongdoing.)

These people could not be blamed for wanting to make more money. I felt those aspirations myself, and would soon pursue them with my own career on Wall Street, though beginning at a much lower level. But to me these moves made the Fed's Men of Silver appear merely mortal. It was as if the system offered such powerful incentives and temptations that no one could resist.

As for Taylor, he remained true until his early death in 1992 at age fifty-three. His track record at the Fed earned him the top spot at another agency, the Federal Deposit Insurance Corporation, where he took a substantial pay cut. The FDIC was insolvent at the time, but he managed to rescue the organization and build its reserves to protect against future bank losses. (Bankers hated the move, predictably enough, because it increased their costs and hurt earnings.) That success may have been a stepping-stone to bigger posts if not for his untimely end, less than four years after I sat with him in the Fed conference room to talk about the Cedar Vale case. Would Bill Taylor have sold out to cash in on his years of public service, as so many others did? Or would he have continued representing higher noble interests? I'd like to think he would have steadfastly held to the ideals of public service, stayed away from the revolving door between the private and public sectors, and remained a civic leader to the very end.

Chapter 2

The Big Time—or Something Like It

By my fifth year at the Fed, in 1992, I was ready to go. I felt like I had learned what I could there, and I still wanted to get to Wall Street. I was young and I had the desire to be in the center of things. I needed to prove that the people who had dismissed me were wrong, and, to be honest, I wanted to make some money. I remember watching *Wall Street* and hearing Gordon Gekko tell the Bud Fox character about all the money he could make: "I'm talking about liquid. Rich enough to have your own jet. Rich enough not to waste time. Fifty, a hundred million dollars, buddy."

I had been busting my butt for years. While at IBM, I woke up at 5 A.M. to work out, went to my full-time job, and then pursued my MBA at night, finishing the degree in under three years. I had also studied for my chartered financial analyst (CFA) certification, which is de rigueur for a serious Wall Street contender. The CFA is a complicated

endeavor—a series of three, increasingly difficult yearly exams covering a broad financial curriculum, including ethics. Either you passed
and moved on to the next level, or you failed and waited one full year
before getting a chance to try again.

By the time I was studying for the third and final exam, in 1990,
I was dating a woman, Jackie, whom I had met playing paddleball at
Dewey Beach, Delaware, in the summer of 1990. My friends joked
when we met that I found her attractive in part because she could cor-
rectly identify who Alan Greenspan was. She knew how important the
CFA was to me and was willing to put up with my extreme notions of
preparedness. I asked her to carry flash cards with various CFA topics
and quiz me repeatedly. Despite this chore, she is now my wife and
has been putting up with me ever since. After I got through the CFA
process, I wanted to take the next step.

The job-search process again proved to be frustrating, and it reinforced my notion that some people were insiders on Wall Street and
I was not. From the Fed library, I looked at back issues of *Institutional
Investor Magazine*, especially those that included the magazine's annual
list of "All Star Analysts" in each sector. I wanted to work for the
best. I put together a list of bank analysts and started cold-calling
them. Part of my strategy involved timing: I figured that administrative assistants would be leaving each day at 5:00, so I called right
around 5:05. If the Fed fax machine was tied up I'd wait, because I
wanted to make sure I'd be able to send a resume right away, though
I always offered to travel up to New York and hand-deliver one, as
well. The phone system we had would ring once for Fed calls and
twice for external calls—this was before cell phones—and I had left
so many messages at Wall Street firms that I jumped every time my
phone rang twice.

After weeks of effort, cold-calling more than twenty analysts, I
finally got my first Wall Street interview. Perceptions were still against
me though. "We work hard here," the interviewer told me. "At the
government, I imagine it's 9 to 5. Not so here. You work, and then in
your free time, you work some more." I couldn't quite convince him
that I'd been working hard for seven years, logging eighteen-hour days
and shuffling multiple responsibilities to finish my master's degree and
earn the CFA designation while working full time.

Years later, after I was firmly situated in a Wall Street job, I'd remember those words—*We work hard here*—and wonder why the interviewer couldn't separate my potential from my lack of pedigree. The words would occur to me when I was at the office on a Sunday at 3:00 P.M. in August, or on the morning of New Year's Day, or the Friday after Thanksgiving. I would be alone, or with Jackie. She was in graduate school at the time, and she'd sit at an adjacent cubicle studying biochemistry or pathology. The copier was in energy-saving mode and would take five minutes to warm up again when I needed it—even the *copier* took days off. Afterward, we would treat ourselves to dinner at our favorite greasy Chinese noodle shop at the corner of 49th and Second.

I had a surreal interview experience at First Boston, which later became part of Credit Suisse First Boston. *Institutional Investor* ran an article about Tom Hanley, a genuine Power Broker and one of the most connected people on Wall Street. Hanley had worked at Salomon Brothers for more than twenty years, and he was named one of *Institutional Investor*'s "All-Star Analysts" for eight years straight. He published lists of potential takeover targets in the bank industry, and he was uncannily accurate. The article in *Institutional Investor* described how Hanley had shown up for work at Salomon Brothers and been kicked out of the building at 6:30 A.M., before he'd finished his first cup of coffee. He wasn't even allowed to return to his office to retrieve the extra socks he kept at his desk. His crime? Hanley was considering another job offer he'd received, from First Boston, for a reported $2 million a year. There were rumors he had also tried to take some of his staff with him, which his bosses at Salomon found objectionable. I was fascinated by this rough-and-tumble world of Wall Street where, on one hand, the Power Broker could take home a seven-figure salary and, on the other hand, be thrown out of the building at the first hint of lost loyalty.

When he got up and running at First Boston, Hanley had his own team of five analysts, so I thought there might be room for me. I called him repeatedly, faxing my resume several times, until finally I was granted an interview. Before meeting him, I sat down with his assistant, who showed me research they had done. It contained extremely detailed insights into the strategy of JPMorgan, projections of revenues and earnings, and perspectives with the kind of detail I had never generated at the Fed. The work was fantastic, and I wasn't sure if I could do something at that level. Not until later did I understand that many of the charts were taken straight from JPMorgan's formal presentation to analysts, as was customary. The First Boston team wasn't coming up with new information as much as passing along data given to them by the companies.

The assistant then told me about Hanley's broad reach. "Tom is one of the most powerful people on Wall Street," he said. "He moves business. All he had to do was mention that he was switching firms, and the business of NationsBank [today Bank of America] moved along with him." Next the assistant ushered me into the Power Broker's cavernous office, large enough that it took me a few long seconds to make my way from the door to his desk. I gave him a firm handshake (something I had literally practiced with roommates—solid grip, not too tight, eye contact, smile a little but don't grin), and started on my pitch: "Worked my way through school, toiled at the Fed, got my professional certifications, worked very hard."

About five minutes in, Tom Hanley said, "You've got the job." That was it. I remembered reading that the most successful executives knew how to make decisions instantly, as I had read in the book *The One Minute Manager*, and I thought that I just witnessed this firsthand. Finally, someone could see the things that I saw in myself. He walked me out of his office and instructed me to come back to see his boss, but noted that this would only be a formality.

As soon as I got back to Washington, I enlisted my mom to help me pick out a diamond ring I could give to Jackie. This was big—I had read about the four C's of diamonds—cut, color, clarity, carat weight—and my mom arranged to have a diamond dealer and regular customer of her and my stepdad's restaurant, the Vagabond, bring in a few samples to show me at the bar. I picked one out and spent about $4,000, a third of my net worth at the time. To me, the job offer was the first domino that I needed to fall before everything else: getting married, moving to New York, Jackie starting medical school. I couldn't wait to tell the breakfast table that I would soon be working for the number-one bank analyst on Wall Street. It was like getting picked to join the Yankees.

Everything was falling into place—except that it wasn't. A week later, I was back in New York for the follow-up interview, much more confident and less anxious about my handshake technique. My only meeting was with Tom Hanley's boss at First Boston. It was just to finalize the details, or so I thought.

But right away the tone was different. This man was more formal. He kept his jacket on. He had gray hair and a demeanor that reeked of old-school Wall Street partnerships. "Tom has his own deal at the firm and runs somewhat independently," he started off, "but I'm the research director." This seemed like my invitation to speak. I gave my fought-through-the-trenches pitch again. Then he was silent. I shifted positions in my chair. More silence. "We only hired two people this year," he finally said. "One from Stanford and one from Harvard." And then he stood up. Another five-minute interview, with a different result.

I didn't understand, and it wasn't until I got back to Washington that the harsh fact that I didn't have the job started to settle in. But how could that be? The most powerful analyst on Wall Street told me I had the job. We shook hands on it. A handshake should be as good as a contract. Still, I wasn't ready to give up. If I didn't have a job, I could at least get an explanation. I started calling, every day or two, and I didn't stop until I got Tom Hanley on the phone again. It took me almost three weeks. He simply said that it wasn't going to happen. No explanation. No apology. Jackie pretty quickly understood what this meant. It was back to dollar-drink nights, half-price burgers, and biking through Rock Creek Park. As for the diamond ring, my mother held it, in confidence, for yet another day.

I met someone years later who told me out of the blue that he'd had an almost identical experience with Tom Hanley—a short inter-view, a handshake, the effusive "You're in," only to have the firm later rescind the offer. We agreed that it was probably just a power game for him. Hanley had a long and impressive career on Wall Street, but he received some black eyes along the way. In 1997, he would spread rumors that Bankers Trust was a potential takeover target and would likely be bought by Travelers Group. That rumor caused BT's stock to soar—the company's market value jumped by more than $1 billion, until trading in the stock was halted. As it turned out, the rumor was false. A week later, Travelers bought Salomon instead. It might have been an honest mistake, but Hanley happened to have a very good friend, who happened to invest Hanley's own stock portfolio, primarily in bank stocks, and the money manager made a nice sum of money based on that false rumor. The New York Stock Exchange ended up fining Hanley $75,000 over the incident, but he remained connected to Wall Street.

In the two decades since then, I've followed the careers of some of the other people I interviewed with during that period, when I was so desperate to get to Wall Street. One executive at boutique brokerage firm Keefe Bruyette and Woods was extremely nice to me when we met; tragically, he died in the World Trade Center attacks on 9/11. The CEO with whom I met at Keefe was convicted for passing inside information about upcoming bank mergers to his porn-star mistress, who made $88,000 on the arrangement. Though he was worth more than $10 million, the executive was convicted for insider trading and ended up serving time.

At last, in 1992, I landed a job as a junior analyst at Union Bank of Switzerland (UBS). It had taken me seven years, including eight months of active job searching in this phase alone, plus countless letters and cold calls, and a few false starts, but I'd finally made it. I was in the club— finally on Wall Street.

I got the job offer on a Friday and immediately accepted. I took Jackie to the Inn at Little Washington, one of the best restaurants in the DC area, where I'd somehow managed to finagle a last-minute reservation. I already had the ring, so that night I proposed. She was working at the National Institutes of Health in DC at the time while applying to medical schools in New York City. Life was starting to come together.

At the time, UBS was a small firm in the United States. It had maybe fifteen senior analysts on a single small floor at its headquarters on Park Avenue and 48th Street. But I soon realized that I was still an outsider. UBS wasn't one of the main firms on the Street, and I was a low-ranking employee there.

My boss at UBS was a character, outspoken and with a raucous, baudy sense of humor. He kept a can of Spotted Owl Soup prominently displayed on a shelf in his office, a joke referring to his disdain for the environmental movement. He had an office that overlooked the rooms at the InterContinental Hotel, and when a woman appeared in one of the hotel windows, he shouted to let us all know. I sat in a cubicle outside his office and sometimes ran personal errands for him, like fetching his dry cleaning. During my first week on the job he took me to his "club," the University Club, where we played squash. Men there swam naked—I had no idea that this took place in the twentieth century. My boss put me up at the club for a weekend before I found my own place. Because my wife and I were dressed so casually, we were told to use the service entrance.

Finally, we found a tiny studio apartment at East 81st Street and Third Avenue, which we only later learned had a prostitute living down the hall and mice scurrying inside the walls. It cost $900 a month. I'm an efficiency nut, so I timed whether it was faster to take the local train from 77th Street and Lexington or backtrack to 86th to catch an express. (Answer: 77th, but just barely. I took my wife on these time trials, and she was not pleased with the experience.)

It was fortunate that I received some training in financial analysis at the Fed, because I got little on the job. Before getting to Wall Street, I was amazed by the way analysts could publish such precise, insightful reports on the companies they covered. I thought they must just be amazingly talented at their jobs. But that wasn't it—they were getting their information directly from the companies, often in winks and nods during private meetings with management. In some cases, analysts would show their spreadsheets to a bank's CFO and ask what he thought. The CFO would point to a certain column and say, "Hmmm, that seems a little conservative to me." The analyst would put a new number in and look expectantly at the CFO, who would smile. Message received. This wasn't analysis but simply forwarding a company's information to their clients.

In August 2000, the Securities and Exchange Commission would adopt a rule called Regulation FD, or "Fair Disclosure," to stop that kind of information seepage. Reg FD prevents public companies from revealing important information to select people in individual meetings like this—if it's material info, it has to go out to everyone. Reg FD is a great rule.

Back in the 1990s, however, the rule wasn't in place yet, and Wall Street analysts still got much of their information spoon-fed to them from management. That wasn't the kind of work I wanted to do. Instead, I wanted to dig into the financials and spot things that no one else had seen. To that end, I came up with a new model for valuing banks, calling it an "adjusted book value model" and later a "bank franchise value model." This approach involved going through a bank's balance sheet and correcting each line item, up or down, for everything you could possibly know about it.

At the Fed, this type of technique was largely restricted to capital and reserves, since those were the elements that kept banks from going under. But, I thought, why stop there? What about unfunded pension plans and unrealized gains on business lines, tax credits, and everything else? Why not include everything you could possibly put a value on, including some subjective items? The old method was a little like pricing a house based on square footage and nothing else, while not recognizing that some houses have pools, upgraded kitchens, new roofs, or are in great school districts.

The approach didn't seem extremely radical to me but was considered a big advance for the process of analyzing banks. We explained our formula, kept everything transparent, and advanced the thinking on how to value bank stocks just a little bit. If someone else thought that one of the adjustments was wrong, we could immediately adjust the formula and give a new result. No one else was doing that kind of work on banks. Less than a year after I arrived, I put out my first report that valued banks using this model, and *Forbes* soon published my results even though I was a Wall Street rookie.

■ ■ ■

I did learn some things from my boss at UBS, though, things that you don't pick up in business school. First, as he put it, "take a stand, and then find reasons to support it." He wanted me to be bold and take action, and he said it was more important to be loud than to be right. I wasn't sure I agreed with this latter point. To me, the accuracy of my research mattered more—or at least, it *should* matter more. I wanted to be methodical and systematic and to find out things that would genuinely impact the value of a bank stock over time. That was how, I thought, an analyst would represent value for clients.

But I wasn't inclined to raise these arguments. I was just a neophyte—what did I know?

The second thing my boss emphasized was that you should party with clients in social settings. Beer and steak, he felt, can mean more to some clients than the work itself. After one bank conference in Florida, we threw a big poker party in his room. We brought in chips and vodka and iced down cases and cases of beer. By the end of the night, he literally had to be carried out, which helped to score points with clients.

Perhaps most important in my growing education about the ways of Wall Street, my boss taught me about the Number. At one point, early on in my time at UBS, I wandered into his office and found him talking with Doug, a Wall Street veteran from the 1970s and 1980s who sported graying hair, a monogrammed shirt, gold cuff links, and a Rolex. My boss said, "I think I can get to the Number."

As the neophyte, I had to ask what this meant. When he didn't answer, Doug explained, "The Number is an amount of money after which you no longer need more money." He said something about limousines and an apartment on Park or Fifth Avenue and a home in the Hamptons. I asked, "How much is that?" They ignored me and moved on to another topic. I was thirty years old and had never considered the concept of acquiring an amount of money so large that you didn't need to think about it anymore. While working as a computer analyst at IBM, the best I could hope for was to increase my salary by a paltry amount with each promotion. At the Fed, pay hikes weren't much easier to secure.

But this was another kind of experience, where I was still torn between competing goals. I didn't think there had to be a dichotomy between material success and the sense I got at the Fed of being a warrior of capitalism. I wanted to be a cross between Gordon Gekko and the Men of Silver—I wanted it both ways, which is easier said than done. There's so much money on Wall Street that it's easy to lose your way.

■ ■ ■

These lessons were brought home by a pair of experiences that showed me the potential reward and punishment of certain actions. I got my first taste of bank backlash at UBS, when I wrote a mildly negative report about KeyCorp. It was the first company I ever met with as a full-fledged bank analyst. The company is still around today—it owns KeyBank and it's headquartered in Cleveland, though its stock has performed pretty badly all these years. As of late 2011, adjusted for splits, shares traded at about half of where they did when I wrote my report almost twenty years ago.

At the time, it was considered an acquisition machine, and most other analysts loved the company. I couldn't help but notice, as I published in a report back then, that this "acquisition machine" had really completed only two major deals—both with the help of the federal government—which were unlikely to be repeated. It had also bought the leftover pieces from a deal involving two other banks, in which they sold some branches after their own merger. To me, two deals plus some scraps did not constitute an acquisition machine. The perception didn't match the reality. I thought: What am I missing?

If you read my report today, it's pretty tame—it says that the company would have a hard time growing and that other banks were better investments. But KeyCorp was not happy. It cut off its banking business with UBS. I heard rumors that some of the more senior people at KeyCorp had taken my report around to some other analysts at competing firms and asked them to write something different. I could never confirm this, but even the rumors were unsettling. This was my initiation into the big time: Say something that a bank doesn't like, and it will retaliate, even if the reasoning is correct.

Around that same time, I experienced the other side of this phenomenon as well. After I recommended the stock of Bank One (today part of JPMorgan), my boss said that I needed to take its CEO, John McCoy, around to see our investors, who often pay for this type of exclusive access. In other words, as long as I think that the stock is a "buy," I should see what the company would do to help UBS. It was an implicit—and sometimes explicit—type of quid pro quo.

I obliged and asked John McCoy if he would join me in meeting some investors. First it was a lunch in New York City for local clients. That went well, and I asked if he would be willing to travel to meet some other clients around the country. Not only did he accept, but he offered to fly me to Los Angeles on Bank One's corporate jet. Our wives would come, too. It was my first and only flight on a private jet.

I had always noticed the many exits off the airport road before the main terminal and wondered what they were used for.

We met the CEO and his wife at the airport and climbed aboard the Gulfstream. No crowds. No hassle. No fixed takeoff time—it was like the airborne equivalent of a limo. (Years later I would hear another bank CEO answer a question about when his flight took off by saying "When I get there.") We had drinks and shrimp cocktail and a dinner heated up in the galley by John McCoy himself. A big-shot CEO, *serving me dinner*. My wife has always hated flying, but after he took her to the cockpit, where she sat with the pilot and learned how the plane worked, she felt safe in the air for the first, and only, time.

During my entire time at the Fed, I had never met a CEO from a major bank. I rarely talked to anyone within management—we almost always spoke through lawyer intermediaries. And, John McCoy was one of the most popular CEOs in the industry. *American Banker*, the trade paper that I always saw weeks late at the Fed, named him "Banker of the Year" in 1992. Yet here I was, a guest on a private jet, having hours of one-on-one access, all because of a positive rating. I could ask him informal questions about the company's strategy, the impact of events in Congress, the future potential of China—anything I wanted. Shrimp cocktail *and* access.

At one point, he told me that the Gulfstream had been picked up in bankruptcy, or something along those lines. I understood his point—he didn't want to see details of the company's private jet in my next research report. The unspoken agreement was that you were expected to abide by the gentlemanly rules. Fly on the CEO's jet but do not make disparaging remarks. Get an edge on the upcoming earnings but do not make critical comments about the firm's strategy.

One of the biggest surprises from the trip came after I got back home. I returned to our studio apartment to find a voice message waiting: "Hello, Mike and Jackie, it's John McCoy. Thank you for a great trip!" He had tracked down our home phone number and called to thank us, even though it should have been the other way around. The contrast could not have been more stark—we were home, in our place with the mice in the walls, having just stepped down from a Gulfstream a few hours earlier. This came two years into my Wall Street career.

I had finally arrived, and I was learning about the prizes that awaited if the banks liked what you had to say.

■ ■ ■

Just as significantly, I learned some things about the culture of high finance during my time at UBS. Guys like my boss back then are a familiar type on Wall Street—they're backslappers, lots of fun. He allowed me to initiate coverage on banks that were below the radar screen for him. Shawmut Bank was one of my first; it later merged with Fleet and is now part of Bank of America. I remember the morning we opened coverage. The report went out to clients, and we started watching the ticker. He was cheering for me: "Stock's up a quarter, stock's up a half. Go, Shawmut, go!" It felt good to have him pulling for me like that.

But even at this early point in my career, I realized that in many ways I was different from my boss and many of his colleagues, who would not hesitate to start off a meeting with an off-color joke about flight attendants. For better or for worse, I'm not part of that crowd. When I got married, I didn't invite anyone from my job to the wedding. I wanted to keep that part of my life separate, and I've continued that throughout my career. More important, guys like that boss didn't seem likely to take a strong stand solely on principle. If it earned them a bigger bonus, definitely. But on ethical considerations? I don't know. Maybe I realized this only after I'd left UBS, when apparently my old boss co-opted the model I'd come up with to predict likely bank takeovers, as if he'd done all the work himself. It sure didn't seem fair.

This would not be the last time that some of my colleagues on Wall Street acted less than ethically. Over time, I would have other ideas borrowed from me—sometimes small stuff, like a chart I'd put together; sometimes larger things, like an entire valuation model. My sense of outrage whenever these things have happened has never really worn off. If people were willing to do this to me, someone that they knew and had worked with for years, just to gain a very minor advantage at their jobs, what would they do to clients, investors and other people they might not have ever met in person, in situations where the stakes—and potential gains—were so much higher?

■ ■ ■

After two years at UBS, in 1994, I was ready to move on. Lehman Brothers had rejected me when I was at the Fed, saying I didn't have any experience, so after two years at UBS, I called the head of research and said, "Now I have some experience. Can I come work for you?" Astonishingly, it worked.

I later found out that Lehman had checked me out before hiring me by calling the companies I covered to ask their opinion of me. At the time I remember thinking: Why does their opinion matter? It was another example of insiders conferring with each other to decide if I was worthy. My objective was to serve the clients—the investors who owned stock in these banks—and not the banks themselves.

Unlike UBS of the early 1990s, Lehman was the big time, one of the highest-profile firms on Wall Street. It was ranked number one in research and had swarms of deal makers and traders, all in its headquarters at the World Financial Center. I felt as though I had transferred from community college to a large university. At Lehman, I had my own space, next to the offices of the other seven financial analysts. I could even hire an associate to help me with some of the grunt work inherent to my job. One person I interviewed offered to work for free for three months, at which point I could decide if I wanted to bring him on officially. I hired him on the spot, with pay.

I loved the work I was doing in my new job, but there were some aspects of the culture where I just didn't fit in. This was brought home to me once at a party hosted by one of our clients at Lehman. It was at his weekend home out in Water Mill, New York, near the Hamptons. Jackie and I were ridiculously underdressed. Other guests were wearing monogrammed long-sleeve shirts, a few with blue blazers, and one even had wingtips on. Jackie and I were used to the parties at Dewey Beach, where you showed up to parties in a bathing suit, and if you wanted to be a little dressy, you put a neon T-shirt over it. We had a hard time striking up a conversation—everyone seemed cold and inaccessible.

Finally we found someone nice. He chatted with us for about ten minutes and then said he was sorry but he had to get back to work. He was one of the bartenders.

There was protocol that I was tripping through at work, too. To evaluate a company called the National Bank of Detroit, I flew out to Michigan and met with its executives. I asked what I thought were pretty straightforward questions (as in "If the auto cycle slows, are you prepared for reduced growth?"). But a few days later, back in New York, I was called in by my boss—the bank had called Lehman to complain that my questions were too tough and accusatory. I was summoned to a high floor in the building to meet with a senior executive at Lehman whom I'd never heard of. He was a former auto firm CEO and worked at Lehman solely to generate banking business with the auto industry. He was a rainmaker, little more.

The man was personable in an aristocratic sort of way, and I felt like an unwashed immigrant coming straight from Ellis Island to meet with Henry Ford himself. His message was clear: I shouldn't annoy the people at these banks. I should try to be a little more gentle and lay off the tough questions. Lehman, amazingly, forced me to fly back out to Detroit for a do-over of the meeting with National Bank of Detroit, to show them my softer side.

If I found this troubling, there were lots of perks to distract me. Only one week after joining Lehman, the firm hosted a conference for investors in Bermuda. Meetings were in the mornings, and afternoons were set aside for golf, snorkeling, swimming, and hanging out with frozen drinks. Dinners were buffets of lobster, shrimp, fresh amberjack, and mackerel. My golf foursome won the low score, and, more important, I won the long drive contest for the only time in my life. Jackie came with me on the trip, and I remember looking at her at dinner one night and we both knew what the other person was thinking: Is this real? Are we actually here right now, experiencing this? We were brought back to Earth by the evening's entertainment, the strains of the 1950s R&B band, Little Anthony and the Imperials.

Some of the other client entertainment was decidedly less family friendly. During one trip to Minneapolis to see investors, one of the Lehman salesmen took me around to see the firm's main accounts for the better part of a day, where I discussed my valuation model for banks.

That night, after a steak dinner, we all piled into a car and ended up at a bar in the city's warehouse district, where lines of naked women were dancing inside. The salesman supplied hundred-dollar bills to the clients for lap dances, and some of the clients disappeared with the dancers into a booth in the back for more private entertainment. I sipped beer with the clients who lingered on the fringes, naively wondering which was likely to have more of an effect on the clients: my research or a hundred-dollar bill given to them to hand to strippers. I got back to my hotel at 2:00 A.M. and was up early the next morning for meetings. When I offered to chip in to pay for my share of the beer, the salesmen told me he would write the whole thing off as a business expense— "entertainment."

■ ■ ■

But my bigger missteps had to do with my interactions with the investment bankers at Lehman. At the big banks around this time, analysts were specifically tasked with supporting the investment bankers, the deal makers in charge of gaining business from the companies that we researched. That kind of collaboration isn't allowed anymore, but back in the mid-1990s, it was prevalent on Wall Street, and Lehman was no different. The bankers were constantly trying to do deals—secondary stock offerings, bond issuances, mergers, buyouts—and thus earn fat fees. As analysts, we were expected to help them. The thinking was that if we said something positive about the companies in our sector, we'd curry favor with them, and they'd choose our bankers to do their next deal. If we said something honest but less than flattering . . . well, I would soon find out.

The investment bankers had a weekly lunch to discuss strategy and potential new clients, and during one of my first months at Lehman, I was invited. Some of the investment bankers at Lehman were straight out of central casting—expensive shoes, French-cuffed shirts, slicked-back hair, suspenders. In an early meeting, they explicitly asked me about John McCoy, the head of Bank One, who had served me shrimp cocktail on his company's Gulfstream. I got the sense that they already knew that I had a decent working relationship with him. It even occurred to me that this was one of the main reasons I was hired at Lehman—to bring Bank One in as an invest-ment banking client.

I told them about my travels with McCoy to Los Angeles to meet with clients, until one of the senior bankers cut through my sentimen-tal tale and said, "That's all good, but how do we turn that warmth into money for the firm?" I pondered those words for a few seconds—*warmth into money*. They were effectively saying, Deliver the goods. Help us get them to do a deal. I told them, frankly, that I had no idea. I didn't think it was my job to drum up mergers and acquisitions business or to convert bank CEOs into clients. After the meeting was over, it dawned on me that I might not thrive at Lehman. But all I could do was focus on my research and analysis, trying to determine which stocks would make good investments.

The same thing happened not long after. I criticized an acquisition made by the bank PNC, and the same investment banker, in the same weekly lunch, shouted at me over the platter of sandwiches: "How do we make money from this?" To many investment bankers, there's no such thing as a bad deal—they *all* generate fees for their firm, even if the cli-ent companies and their investors lose out. To me that didn't make sense. Some clients shouldn't do deals—some deals have no inherent strategic logic. And I was advising a different audience: the investors who owned, or might want to purchase, PNC stock.

Analysts were specifically evaluated by investment bankers back then—it was part of our performance review and part of how our compensation was structured. Favorable marks could improve our pros-pects for advancement within the firm. And, predictably enough, the deal makers gave me one of the lowest marks, saying that I was not a team player.

It didn't seem to make a difference to the firm that my calls regard-ing bank stocks were good, particularly one I made in late 1994. For decades prior to that point, most banks could operate only within a single state—if you wanted to own branches in, say, New York and New Jersey, you needed a separate holding company for each. But in 1994, Congress passed a law striking this rule down. At the time, banks were bogged down in a bear market, but I thought that the new law would mean a wave of consolidation and cost cutting, leading to a boost in stock prices. Banks would face much sharper competition, and they'd have to either perform better or get bought, which would help investors either way.

In December 1994, I put buy ratings on most of the bank stocks I covered. The industry had fallen by 20 percent that year alone, and investors told me that virtually no one agreed with me—not Lehman's senior strategist (a former bank analyst), or the firm's technician (the person tracking stock movements), or any other bank analyst at a major firm except for Credit Suisse analyst Tom Hanley, who was rather muted in his support of bank stocks.

I created a new valuation model, similar to the one I had developed at UBS, this time to predict which banks were likely to be takeover targets. The picks from that model ran in publications like the *Wall Street Journal* and *Barron's*. I was extremely vocal with my bullishness. My public optimism triggered a backlash—one investor said to me, "All you ever say is buy, buy, buy." The good news: The model made accurate predictions. Within a month of my call in December 1994, the stocks in the banking sector turned upward. Over the next few years, the Standard & Poor's (S&P) bank index would go up more than 250 percent. From 1995 to 1999, my picks averaged a 52 percent annual gain, far exceeding the overall market. I was making money for my clients. In 1997, *Institutional Investor* magazine included me in its list of "All-Star Analysts" for the first time, and in 1998, six years into my career, I was named the magazine's top regional bank analyst.

■ ■ ■

To the bankers at Lehman, however, work like this didn't seem to be important. The positive calls weren't generating them any business—in part because I had little inclination to meet with them during those Monday lunches and turn those calls into business—and I still went negative in cases where I thought it was warranted. One example: KeyCorp, the same Cleveland bank where I'd gotten burned at UBS for saying things in a research report that they didn't like. During my first year at Lehman, I put out another report on KeyCorp, called "Honeymoons Don't Last Forever." The title was a reference to the way that the company had been formed by a merger of equal-size companies, which would now be forced to combine their somewhat different cultures and operating styles.

KeyCorp was furious. It would be four years before management at the company would speak to me again. They banned the report inside the company and cut off investment banking business with Lehman. It was like the movie *Groundhog Day*. I didn't like what I saw, and time would prove me right—KeyCorp's stock would be stuck in neutral for more than a year, while the S&P 500 increased by about 25 percent.

My entire time at Lehman was the same story: Produce solid research, and yet it didn't positively impact my performance reviews. In my year-end evaluation, the comments from the deal makers derided my commitment to investors, saying "Mike Mayo will do anything to get ahead . . . and that's not good." I thought that was ironic—I wasn't doing the one thing that would have led to a more successful career at Lehman (i.e., playing nice with the investment bankers) and I clearly wasn't getting ahead within the firm, even though investors rewarded my frank analysis. When the promotions came, I remained not only below the rank of managing director, which connotes one of the top analysts in the field, but below the level of senior analyst, too.

Others were hired above me on my team, people who didn't have the status that I did with investors, and my boss told me that an analyst who had beaten me out for a job at another firm years earlier—at least in part because she'd gone to Harvard—was interviewing to head my team.

I thought, How can I be treated so poorly? My wife has little patience for what happens on Wall Street—to her it's a bunch of entitled people pushing piles of money around. She put it to me simply: "Your job is to make your firm money . . . what do you think?" To that I responded, "Short term or long term?"

I got an opportunity in 1997 to head the bank research team at Credit Suisse First Boston. Interestingly, I interviewed for the spot vacated by power broker Tom Hanley, who had left for UBS, part of the endless musical-chairs element of Wall Street. I jumped at the chance. Giving notice at Lehman was not a pleasant experience. The research director turned stern and escorted me like a sentry immediately back to my office to get my bag. We walked past the offices of colleagues and cubicles of junior staffers, past the reception area, to an awkward wait for the elevator. I stared straight ahead and she said nothing, down the long elevator ride to the marble-encased lobby in the World Financial Center, until I had passed through the turnstiles by the station where the guards kept watch. It felt as though the Lehman deal makers had already escorted me out a few months earlier.

Chapter 3

Exile . . . and Redemption

As my career gained momentum throughout the late 1990s, I got a sense that the stakes were rising in multiple ways. Each job gave me a higher profile on Wall Street, with more seniority and responsibility, and more clients looking to me for the truth about the banking sector. My calls were good, and I believed in the work I was doing. However, the schism between my vision of what Wall Street should look like and the reality of what I saw every day was growing wider. I had a feeling this disparity couldn't last. If I wanted to make sure my job had actual meaning—if I was really going to be objective about what I saw in the banking industry—something would have to give. This all came to a head at my next job, at Credit Suisse First Boston, and it had ramifications that I could never have predicted.

One of the first things I noticed about working at Credit Suisse was that client entertainment was as prevalent as it had been at my earlier firms but was far more lavish. In fact, it began to border on the absurd. The firm would rent a helicopter to ferry managers and clients to golf outings. Credit Suisse analysts could reserve a private dining room in the building to have dinner served by some of the best chefs in New York. While junior analysts were toiling several floors below, sitting in cubicles and crunching spreadsheets, we would be in hushed rooms, clinking silverware with clients. I could invite my wife and six others—sometimes investors who were more friends than clients. The chefs would come out after dinner and give us signed copies of their cookbooks. I saved the menu from one dinner by David Bouley, one of the rock stars of the New York restaurant scene. On gold vellum paper, the menu lists sashimi tuna with key lime–pickled spring Vidalia onion, Chatham lobster, foie gras in poppyseed Armagnac sauce, and, for dessert, something called "tophenstreusel cloud" with wild berries. Wine? Do you even have to ask?

Yet, as I wiped the tophenstreusel crumbs from my mouth after events like this, I was increasingly conflicted, because I knew the source of these perks—the investment bankers again, in the banking sector but primarily in technology. My own work didn't revolve around tech, but Credit Suisse was a major player in the sector, at a time when the NASDAQ was setting records and tech initial public offerings were jumping out of the gate. In 1998, the firm had brought in eighteen tech analysts and their boss, Frank Quattrone. From their arrival in 1998 through 2000, the firm led seventy-nine tech IPOs—three of every four Credit Suisse deals—worth $8.7 billion. The average gain on the first day of trading for those stocks was 93 percent. The result was hundreds of millions in fees for Credit Suisse, and a currency—shares of hot IPO stocks—that could be used to reward clients, pad the compensation of bankers, and tempt other tech CEOs who were about to go public and might be looking for a banker.

I was promoted to managing director at Credit Suisse, the equivalent of partner, and my earlier calls had given me some clout among clients. I thought that I had a good working relationship with the firm's deal makers who arranged big transactions for banks. One of them was Oliver Sarkozy, whose brother, Nicholas, would later become president of France. They didn't pressure me for positive ratings, and I got the sense they genuinely wanted my unbiased opinion. At one point I wrote a report on First Union that was absolutely scathing. But, as opposed to my prior experience, the two lead investment bankers took my report directly to First Union (now part of Wells Fargo) and laid out a case for how the bank needed to fix the problems. First Union agreed with my analysis, and with the bankers' prescription, then hired our firm to do the necessary transactions. That's how the system is supposed to work. No puffery—just clear analysis, in a transparent way. Everyone speaks openly, and the marketplace of ideas decides who's right.

But as analysts and deal makers, we were still significantly over-shadowed by the tech team. When I talked to some of the tech analysts, they treated me as though I were invisible. Once, as I waited outside of a junior Internet analyst's office, he barked, "What do you want?" Another analyst who tracked Internet banks would not return my phone calls; I was told he would only return phone calls to Frank Quattrone and to the *New York Times*.

My peers showed their stripes in other ways, too. At my first—and, as it would turn out, only—conference for managing directors with Credit Suisse, the keynote speaker was Colin Powell, leader of U.S. troops during the first Gulf war and later Secretary of State. During his speech at our conference, some of the managing directors in the back rows were yelling out catcalls to each other, like high school kids during an assembly. I was deeply embarrassed that people at our firm would show such disrespect to this leader and statesman, a man who had worked his way up from the South Bronx.

I managed to keep my outsider status intact, more or less, though occasionally I'd get glimpses of the other side. In 1999, after Credit Suisse brokered a deal in which US Bancorp (then called Firstar) bought Mercantile for $10 billion, the executives of the soon-to-be-merged company held a presentation to formally announce their new strategy. These postdeal presentations are standard operating procedure, in banking or any other sector. The new executives get a large conference room somewhere and shake hands in front of their new logo for photographers and then lay out their vision for analysts, investors, and anyone else with an interest in how the new company is going to operate. The investment bankers are there, too—in some cases having coached the execs to stay on message and highlight the purported benefits of the deal.

I had been to many of these meetings during the banking industry's intense consolidation over the past two decades. But this one was
different. When I got to the lush upper floor of the fancy midtown
hotel, I saw one of our firm's deal makers for the bank sector. He
said, "Here, follow me." Apparently there was a person he wanted me
to meet.

It was a man in one of the aisle seats, someone I'd never seen before.
"This is the compensation expert," the investment banker said. "This is
the person who made the deal happen." Like many firms on Wall Street,
Credit Suisse contracted a person in deals like this whose sole job was
to massage the compensation packages of execs involved in the deal.
Companies can take one-time charges related to a merger, and those
can be written off, meaning deducted against profits. As a result, companies have an interest in throwing as many things as possible into that
"merger-related" category.

I had always wondered how many of those charges were actually related to the merger and how many were things like payments
that would make a CEO, and other senior managers, rich. Now the
investment banker was basically saying that this person played a key
role in finalizing the deal—up there with corporate strategy, "share-
holder value," and the new company's competitive position. It was a
winking acknowledgment that one of the main reasons this merger
could happen was because all the execs got paid.

I was astounded. This was how deals really get done. For those
few seconds—the duration of a handshake—I was on the inside.
And it only reinforced my need to remain an outsider. As I said,
I went to a long string of these presentations, starting in the mid-1990s,
and this was the only time I had a clear glimpse of the role that compensation played in that wave of consolidation. People respond to
incentives, and Wall Street had (and in many ways still has) an incentive scheme that is fundamentally warped, if not broken. CEOs were
sometimes selling their banks simply so they could make money and
cash in, and banks sometimes made acquisitions not because of some
coherent competitive strategy but because it got their managers paid
more. They could negotiate—with the help of investment bankers and
compensation experts—bigger packages for themselves in the murky
category of "employment agreements," deferred benefits, pension plans,

restricted stock, and other goodies, even while they preached to their thousands of employees to watch every penny.

And bank managers weren't the only guilty party. During this period, as the market grew increasingly frothy and tech stocks continued to soar past any rational valuation, it seemed like just about everyone got tempted to take the fast money. Deal makers were getting paid to create quick flipping transactions for increasingly wealthy executives instead of advising them on the best long-term course of action. Analysts were getting paid to be cheerleaders and support deals instead of looking at companies critically. Accountants were getting paid to be consultants instead of examining the books. Stock traders in Wall Street firms generated more in revenue by giving preferred investors stock prices from prior days. Regulators leveraged their relationships into lucrative private-sector jobs, a form of deferred compensation for their prior government work.

All these actions, by a huge number of people, served to inflate the stock market bubble of the late 1990s, which started with technology but then spread to other sectors. This overhyped euphoria amounted to the strongest signal yet that something was wrong with Wall Street. There were problems with analysts, but there were bigger problems with the system as a whole. And I would soon have a chance not only to take a stand but to bet my entire career on my convictions.

■ ■ ■

What gave me perhaps the biggest concern was a sense that stocks within the banking sector were likely to turn downward again. Five years after the interstate banking law of 1994, which allowed banks to operate across state lines, I thought that the easy gains from consolidation were over. In the somewhat overused metaphor of business-speak, the low-hanging fruit had been picked. When banks couldn't maintain their growth momentum through mergers and cost cuts, they took the next logical step—they made more consumer loans. I assumed this meant the quality of those loans would probably decrease, and, in turn, create a greater risk that some of them would result in losses. At the same time, executive pay was soaring, aided by stock options, which had spread from tech start-ups to every other corner of corporate America. Options can be a useful tool, but they can also encourage executives to take on greater risk. This was a decade before compensation issues were deemed one of the main causes of the financial crisis.

Those were two big warning signs, and I had done a tremendous amount of research on the sector in late 1998 and early 1999, so I knew the case was solid. I've always had fun finding the right title for projects like this, and when I published a jumbo, 1,000-page report on the entire banking industry in 1999, I called it "Banks and the Red Queen Effect." That was an Alice in Wonderland reference from *Through the Looking-Glass*, where the Red Queen and Alice have a race in which they're both running but neither one is getting anywhere. When Alice asks how that can be, the Red Queen says, "Now, here, you see, it takes all the running you can do, to keep in the same place. If you want to get somewhere else, you must run at least twice as fast as that!" In other words, banks would have to work harder to maintain their pace. The book included detailed reports of 47 U.S. banks.

There was more. I wasn't just going to go negative on a few main stocks but the entire sector. I didn't think I could find a single winner in the bunch—not one. This was completely the opposite of what most analysts were saying, not just about banks but about all sectors. In decades past, the ratio of buy ratings to sell ratings had not been this lopsided, and in theory it should be roughly 50–50. That seems right, doesn't it? Some stocks go up, some go down, because of the overall market direction or competitive threats or issues specific to each company. In the late 1990s, the ratio was 100 buys or more for every sell. Merrill Lynch had buy ratings on 940 stocks and sell ratings on just 7. Salomon Smith Barney: 856 buy ratings, 4 sells. Morgan Stanley Dean Witter: 670 buys and exactly 0 sells.

Analysts almost never said to sell specific companies, because that would alienate those companies, they would pull business, and the investment bankers would come down hard on the analysts. Say the word "sell" enough times, and you win a long, awkward elevator ride out of the building with your soon-to-be-former boss. And here I was, ready to go negative on the entire sector.

I thought about maintaining a few buy ratings in my report, just to stay safe, but that didn't feel accurate. If I didn't believe the stocks were going to go up—if I wouldn't put my own money in these companies—then how could I tell clients to do so? I was unequivocal on the way up, during the long rally in bank stocks, when my picks doubled and tripled in price, and now I wanted to be unequivocal on the way down.

I got the reports ready, justifications for individual downgrades and the group as a whole. Even Bank One, with my buddy John McCoy at the helm, was in the bunch. The true genius of taking me on his company's private jet ride a few years earlier was that my impending downgrade felt almost like a betrayal, like a personal insult directed at him, rather than an objective and quantifiably defensible stance that I was taking on his company. In other words, it made me feel bad about doing my job.

I also did a few things in my personal life to prepare myself for the worst. I had always lived my life as if my salary and career could end in a single calamitous day, if the market were to go through some vicious, wrenching downturn. When my wife and I bought an apartment, we deliberately chose a condo, which could be rented out if I lost my job, instead of a co-op, which could not. I kept our debt to a minimum, and we lived within our means, saving heavily. We had no children yet, and there weren't any family considerations—if I lost my job and ended up banished from Wall Street, no one in my family would say I shouldn't have blown my opportunity. They wouldn't have told me that I should have simply sat down and shut up.

Yet even then, once all my preparations were in place, I had a hard time dialing up my courage. On May 17, 1999, I was set to pull the trigger on this entire plan and lost my nerve. I had worked so hard to get to this point in my career, and was now earning a multiple of anything that I ever imagined I would make. Was I really ready to risk all that on some kind of abstract principle?

Then it came to me. If I truly wanted to take this action, I might not have another chance. If I didn't go ahead, I would always wonder what might have been. This combination of circumstances was not likely to come around again—a ridiculously frothy market, with boosterish analysts all around me, a solid case for why bank stocks were likely to sag, and a high-profile position at one of the top firms on Wall Street. I remember going to Orioles games when I was a kid on occasional outings with my father, and learning how to keep score on the official baseball stat sheet. A strikeout was recorded as a "K," but if you strike out looking—meaning you don't even swing the third time—it gets logged as a backward "K." I always thought that was worse, and something you wanted to avoid in life. If I struck out, at least I would go down swinging.

■ ■ ■

On May 24, 1999, I woke up at 4:30 A.M., an hour before the alarm clock was scheduled to go off, and went for my customary run. Exercise has always been my cathartic outlet. On some mornings, I would start at First Avenue and run a loop around Central Park, timing myself criss-crossing over streets to beat the traffic lights. (My best time— 53:23.) Other mornings, I might use the gym and do 1,000 sit-ups in six sets. When traveling, I would improvise, literally running around the airport in Frankfurt or doing laps up and down the stairwell in a Boston hotel on a rainy morning if the fitness center had not yet opened. The workouts always remind me that there's a difference between job stress and genuine physical pain. The stereotypical ways that Wall Streeters cope with the pressure—they drink, they have affairs, they cultivate expensive hobbies like collecting cars—don't work for me. Instead, I exercise maniacally.

On this morning, when it was still too dark to venture into Central Park, I ran along the path bordering the East River, from 78th Street down to the helicopter pad at 60th Street and then back, dodging a few homeless people and jumping over a rat or two. I sprinted back up the walkway at 77th, paused at the top to look out over the dark water, and then kept going past the playground and across York Avenue. A cramp was cutting into my side as I finished the four-miler. This was real physical pain. I was ready.

I got to the office at 6:30 A.M., in a dark suit, white shirt, and my favorite tie in a conservative "Reagan" knot. An hour later the firm held its regular morning meeting between analysts and the sales staff. Among eight analysts covering different sectors that morning, I went first. "In no uncertain terms," I said, "sell bank stocks. I'm downgrading the group. Sell Bank One, sell Chase Manhattan . . ." The message went out over the "hoot," or microphone, to more than fifty salespeople in a dozen cities around the world. They in turn would relay my thoughts to more than 300 money managers at some of the largest institutional investment firms in the business, like teachers' pension plans and large mutual funds such as Fidelity.

After the three-minute presentation, I went back to my desk. Safe so far, I thought, and picked up the phone. I started calling some of the biggest banks I had downgraded, to give them a heads-up, along with some of the firm's institutional-investing clients. Not long after that, I was summoned back to the hoot for a special presentation to the sales force, something that had never happened before. They wanted me to clarify my thinking. Did I really mean what I said? Why not just leave the ratings at hold?

I laid out my case again: declining loan quality, excess executive compensation, and headwinds for the industry after five years of major growth driven by mergers. (I also predicted that Y2K technology issues would factor in, and on that count I was wrong.) The bottom line—I thought bank stocks would lag, and I wanted to lock in the gains my earlier calls had made for clients.

The counterattack started almost immediately. One portfolio manager said, "What's he trying to prove? Don't you know you only put a sell on a dog?" Another yelled, "I can't believe Mayo's doing this. He must be self-destructing." One trader at a firm that owned a portfolio full of bank shares—which began falling right after I made the call—printed out my photo and stuck it to her bulletin board with the word "WANTED" scribbled over it. I'd poked a stick into a hornets' nest. That morning, I got a call from a client who runs a major endowment. "Check out the TV," he said. On CNBC, the commentators had picked up on the news and were now mocking me. Joe Kernen joked, "Who's Mike Mayo, and do we know whether he was turned down for a car loan?" I even got an ominous, anonymous voice mail from someone with a strong drawl cautioning, "Be careful with what you say."

My fellow banking analysts lined up to separate themselves from me. Tom Hanley held a conference call with investors in which he derisively referred to me as "Mayo-naise" and said I didn't understand the companies that I was rating. Merrill Lynch's bank analyst held his own conference call to refute my claims. The Wall Street machine was in action, and it had little patience for an outsider who was willing to say something that other people didn't like. Banks and competitors simply couldn't understand my motives. As analysts, our days were supposed to be spent earning more money for clients, not performing some public service endeavor as I did at the Fed.

The reaction from some clients was a little more promising. One called to ask if I really meant it. (I did.) Another told me that it must have taken great "intestinal fortitude" to go public with something like this, which I appreciated.

I went on CNBC that afternoon, and the interviewer asked me flat out if I was worried about the potential backlash. I said, "I have enough confidence in the banks that I feel that they'll let me do my job the way it's supposed to be done." I also gave a prediction regarding the way banks were aggressively increasing their volume of home loans. I said this could lead to trouble if the country experienced a recession that led to problems in the housing market. The result could be "a self-fulfilling prophecy of lower home prices and lower collateral, not to mention unique political fallout." It would take nearly another ten years for those words to be proven true.

That night my wife and I celebrated with dinner at the Pearl Oyster Bar in Greenwich Village. I was happy and exhausted, and felt more free than ever before. I had survived. Jackie, trained as a scientist, failed to see why I should feel so brave. All I'd done was present my insights accurately and honestly. Over dinner, I tried to explain that the rules of the laboratory were not the rules of this game. Bank stocks finished the day significantly down. If they stayed down, I thought that I'd build credibility for the firm and myself and win more than the battle. I'd show that objective analysis had a place on Wall Street.

Yet my quote on CNBC about confidence in the financial system was possibly misplaced. While the accuracy of the call won me points with some clients, others weren't happy. A few stopped doing business with me and Credit Suisse—taking their stock-trading business elsewhere—and later admitted it was because of my call. Even some that didn't take such drastic action didn't want me to succeed, since that would mean that their portfolios, which included bank stocks, would go down in value.

Of course, the banks that I had downgraded were even more furious, and they let me know it. Routine meetings with management are a standard part of my work, yet when I requested these meetings after my call, several banks said no. One investor-relations executive said, "Why should we help an analyst who doesn't understand our story?" The chief legal counsel at another bank demanded a retraction, which he didn't get. Worse, a couple of big institutions in the Midwest and Southeast threatened to cut all ties with Credit Suisse—no more investment banking deals, no more fees. I had anticipated this, but I wasn't sure yet about the extent of the damage. I still had a good relationship with the deal makers at Credit Suisse, but that could change if I started costing them money.

Within a few months, the market began to experience problems. The Standard & Poor's bank index peaked in July 1999 and fell more than 20 percent by the end of the year. Regional banks, in particular, had their worst performance compared to the overall market in half a century. Individual banks were starting to show cracks as well. In late August, Bank One (which had merged with First Chicago a year earlier) announced that it would miss its earnings projections due to slowing growth at its credit card division. The stock dropped by 25 percent, losing $15 billion of its market cap. CEO John McCoy would be gone by the end of the year, by which point the stock had fallen 47 percent from its peak. McCoy later paid me a compliment in a *Fortune* story about my negative call and its aftermath: "Mayo has strong intellect, and he works hard as hell to understand companies. I respect that." However, McCoy also described my call as "dead-ass lucky."

If I thought the reaction from the banks I covered was bad, it was about to get worse, thanks to a development in my own backyard. The financial industry had gone through a huge consolidation wave in the late 1990s, and much of my success had come from accurately predicting takeover targets. In one *Wall Street Journal* article in 1996, I listed ten such companies, and six of them would be taken over in the next three years. Then, in the summer of 2000, this trend came full circle.

In August 2000 my firm, Credit Suisse, announced that it was buying another investment bank, Donaldson, Lufkin, & Jenrette (DLJ). The move would give Credit Suisse greater scale and clout on Wall Street, moving it up in the rankings of major firms. The combined firm would have to shed some people, because it suddenly had two of everything, including two banking analysts. I thought I would be safe, though.

Of the two of us, I had the higher rankings in *Institutional Investor*'s list. I also had decent marks from the investment bankers at Credit Suisse. When I asked, the assistant research director assured me that I would be fine. I started asking for updates every day, and he repeatedly told me there was no word yet.

Then the rumors started, and his tone shifted from ignorance to apology. The combined firm would "probably" keep the DLJ analyst and her team, meaning I would be laid off. When I heard that I hurled my pen across his office and punched a chair, knocking it over. Adding insult to injury was that this was the same Harvard-educated analyst who had beaten me out for a job a decade earlier, during my Fed-based interviewing days, and had nearly become head of my group at Lehman.

I still couldn't believe it would happen, and I went to work every day thinking of things I could do to prevent it. I got a call one day from someone at the Fed who had once reported to the legendary Bill Taylor. It seemed like a good omen, and I hoped that the spirits of the Fed were looking out for me. The agency wanted me to give a presentation to a group of global bank regulators. The subject? Ways to improve information flow and access, in order to help analyze banks around the world.

I gave it my best, thinking that a firm would never fire somebody who had gained this type of stature, especially when the audience included those who regulated Credit Suisse both in the United States and around the world. Afterward, I sent an e-mail to the head of the brokerage firm at Credit Suisse, mentioning the audience for this and attaching a copy of my presentation. He sent back a short e-mail, just three words: "Way to go."

The day of reckoning was getting closer, and going to work each day felt almost surreal. I, of all people, was asked to talk to a group of new employees about the business of equity research. I gave my standard presentation, talking about the need to remain objective and honest. "I'm a testament that you can do your job the way it's supposed to be done and be a survivor," I said. But as the words came out, my eyes welled with tears. I turned to the side, took a few breaths to collect myself, and continued. The truth was catching up to me.

A week later, in September 2000, I was fired, along with my team. It had been sixteen months since I made my negative call, which seemed increasingly accurate with the passage of time. The decision to let me go wasn't based on merit, and it wasn't related to the merger—I was only the second person in decades to be so highly ranked in both of *Institutional Investor*'s bank categories, and I was fired anyway. I was also the only managing director in the equities department to get the ax. The person who I believe approved my firing, who was then head of equities, today serves as CEO of all of Credit Suisse worldwide.

I always knew that making a big, bold call that turned out to be wrong might cost me my job. I also knew that the deal makers could force me out if I cost them business. As it turned out, my negative call on banks was correct, and I was fired anyway. After working so hard for seven years to get to Wall Street and hustling for another eight once there to do the best work I could, I was out.

■ ■ ■

Over the following six months, I went through all the stages of grief and probably even invented some new ones. On my last day at the firm, I had sent out an e-mail and blast voice message to more than 1,000 investors to announce that I'd been replaced, fantasizing that maybe some of them would demand that I get my job back. I got fifty or so responses during those first few jobless days, offering support and references in my job search, but few of those people reached out to my old boss, and if they did, it didn't make a difference.

I also called the Fed, thinking that they could maybe deny the merger on the grounds that it wasn't in the public interest. This was one of the factors we had looked at back when I worked there. The Men of Silver at the Fed, I thought, would rise up and protect one of their own. These calls went nowhere though. I even called the Securities and Exchange Commission with a question: If I had performed my job by the book and a company blacklisted or bad-mouthed me—or my own firm fired me—would there be any recourse? It was a somewhat naive question, and I knew the answer before I even asked: No, there was no recourse. The Credit Suisse/DLJ merger moved ahead. I would not be getting my old job back. My fantasy died.

For a few weeks, I was obsessed with the fact that I never heard the name of the specific person who had made the decision. It was a committee, a collective "they." One day, as I drove to meet my jobless bank team for a morale-boosting round of golf at New Jersey National, I called, against my better judgment, the head of equities at Credit Suisse. I got his assistant, who told me—remarkably—that he would take the call. I waited about ten seconds, driving down the highway, thoughts racing, and then hung up. I was like the dumped boyfriend, begging for his girlfriend to give him one good reason why she wouldn't take him back.

American Banker ran an article in which the DLJ bank analyst commented about her negative view on banks. In response, I told a reporter that it was as if she not only moved into my old neighborhood but also entered my house and took over my possessions. I wasn't expecting the reporter to print the comment and, later, I called the analyst to tell her this. She was a good sport, saying that she appreciated the phone call, and even gave me some leads for new jobs.

With time, I began to realize that none of these individuals was really to blame. They could have been replaced with a different set of people and the result would have been the same—I still would have been out. There was no conspiracy, and it wasn't personal. The system on Wall Street has been structured so that people are willing to maximize short-term profits and their own paychecks while disregarding the sustainability of their particular approach or the longer-term impact on the firm. It's not capitalism but an amped-up, ravenous version of capitalism. I was out not because someone had it in for me but because I was on the wrong side of this mind-set. Maybe this was the stage known as acceptance. If so, it didn't feel like it to me—I was still furious about everything.

During the warmer fall months of late September and October, I made the best of my time off, meeting the other people from my unemployed team for lunches and rounds of golf. Everyone else was working, we told ourselves, and here we were, out here in the sun. But as Thanksgiving rolled around and the weather turned colder, the experience became a little less fun. Lacking any real purpose, all that time started to weigh on us. I remembered the talk about the Number, the amount of money a person would need to sock away to leave Wall Street forever. Could that really be enough for some people? What would they do all day?

I started to find myself dozing on the couch at 2:00 P.M., in front of a blaring television. Once I was woken by a phone call—a voice I didn't recognize. "I was sleeping," I mumbled. "Who is this? After I hung up, my wife, hearing the one-sided conversation and alarmed by my blurting out that I had been asleep, asked me who the caller was. It was, I told her, John Kanas, the CEO of North Fork Bank, one of the larger U.S. banks at the time, who called to say that he supported my work and wished me luck. Another afternoon on the couch, I was awakened to find Jamie Dimon calling me. Dimon had spent years at Citi with Sandy Weill before being kicked out at the number-two spot, and he had taken over the CEO job at Bank One, replacing John McCoy. This time I heeded my wife's warning to answer in a more alert, and potentially employable, fashion. Dimon gave some words of support and mentioned that his company had a venture capital business in New York City, if I needed a job. I replied that I intended to remain a research analyst but thanked him nonetheless. I couldn't help noticing that some of the more adept CEOs would make calls like this: small, thoughtful gestures as a way to invest their time.

Gradually, I started to take on small projects, just to stay active, and began to write the memoir of my career. To keep up with the industry, and with money out of my own pocket, I traveled around the country to meet with banks—at least, the ones that would see me. I even brought some of my old clients with me, as a way to maintain relationships and goodwill. Trying to network my way to another job, I called everyone I had ever known, which was humiliating at times. A few firms met with me but told me explicitly that their deal makers had concerns. "We're not sure you're 'banker-friendly,'" they said. Code for: You won't play the game. I landed an interview at one firm, only to find that it was with my old boss at Lehman, the woman who had escorted me out of the building. I was nervous, but she was extremely gracious and even gave me a hug. She didn't have spots for my team, but she pointed me to some other people. The search continued.

Not all my experiences were as cordial. A hedge fund gave me a short-term assignment: to attend the Goldman Sachs banking conference in New York and write up my findings. I would have gladly paid to attend this event—all the major banks and CEOs would be there—but instead the hedge fund was paying me to do it. It was December 2000 and I'd been out of a job for three months, but for a few days, at least, I would be back in the game. I entered the Pierre Hotel and gave a woman at the registration desk my name. She immediately told me to leave. I responded, "I'm sorry, but you've made a mistake. I work for an important client and I—"

"*Please leave*," the woman said.

If I hadn't been so down and out I could have managed a joke like "I've been kicked out of better conferences," but I felt humiliated. The entire industry was here, and again I was the outsider, a foreigner, not even told to use the side door this time but simply to get out. I called the hedge fund, and they told me to wait. They made some phone calls, and an hour later I was back at the Pierre. I would be allowed in this time, the Goldman staff people said, but I'd need an escort, who had to stay by my side during the entire event. When I found out that the person was the second-level person covering the hedge fund, I joked that it would take the first string to keep up with me. Nevertheless, I got my information, helped out the hedge fund, and stayed current on the industry.

Even with projects like this, there was an excess of downtime. On my wife's days off we went to movies or coffee bars in the East Village, or simply took long walks. I don't think she fondly recalls this as quality time with me—I was not the most engaging companion at the time. I couldn't avoid the sense that everyone else had something to do, some kind of purpose, and I didn't. Most of my days had no meaning. If this was a preview of retirement, I didn't want it.

The highlight of this period was that I got to spend plenty of time with our oldest daughter, who was an infant then. I had never even held a baby until she was born, and I had no idea what it was like to care for one. We went to classes like Broadway Babies, where out-of-work Broadway performers sang songs with the babies and caregivers. Another class was "Hands On," which had musical instruments for the babies to bang and gnaw. At these classes I would usually be the only dad—just me, maybe two mothers, and about six nannies. I wanted to announce to everyone: *I have a career. I work. This is just temporary.* Instead I played with Lily and sang our songs: "Hands On, Hands On, we all sing together. Hands On, Hands On, we'll have some fun today." Very little of this six-month period was fun for me, but the time with my daughter definitely qualified.

■ ■ ■

Finally, the job search turned in my favor, in a way that worked out better than anything I could have hoped for. I got a call from Prudential Securities, asking if I wanted to come for an interview. I almost turned it down—I had read newspaper accounts of the firm recently firing people. As I learned in an initial meeting, those layoffs were intended to reposition the firm away from investment banking and toward pure research. The interviewer asked me what I thought about that strategy. "Firing a thousand deal makers?" I said. "That's a good start."

In February 2001, after six months of exile, I took the job. My mandate at Prudential was clear: to lead the charge as the firm repositioned away from deals and back to research. I was a warrior of capitalism again. Analysts would be free to say what they wanted about the companies they covered, with no fear of retribution or losing business. If our results were good, we thought, we could help transform the idea of equity research on Wall Street. I felt as though a fairy godmother had granted my wish—my negative call from almost two years earlier was only looking better with the passage of time, and I was back to doing what I loved.

There was more. At the time, I worried that working at Prudential would lower my profile, given that it was a second- or third-tier firm. Instead, Prudential wanted me to be the spokesman for its television commercials. I would be the poster boy for balanced research.

We had no script for these commercials—I merely had to respond ad hoc and on-camera to questions. It was pretty easy, as I had dreamed for years about saying these things to the world. In one spot, I said, "No more mealy-mouth, mumbo jumbo, political-speak type of research . . . take a stand. Mean what you say and say what you mean. Be objective, and balanced, and make investors money." The commercials got a wide release, and even aired during the Kentucky Derby and the NBA finals that year, when the Lakers beat the 76ers. Everyone saw them—family, friends, colleagues, competitors, deal makers, CEOs, and the occasional complete stranger who would, to my wife's chagrin and embarrassment, recognize me in a restaurant. Before a conference call, the head of the law firm Sullivan and Cromwell said, "I saw you during the NBA championship game last night." All that I could say was, "Did you see when my elbows hit the rim?" I was having fun, getting paid for the chance to rant a little about the ridiculous nature of the system on Wall Street. Because it felt like such easy money, I donated all of my commercial payments directly to charity.

Prudential was leading a shift that was starting to spread through the rest of Wall Street, as other firms changed their rating schemes. Even Credit Suisse followed along and emphasized more independent stock research. I would like to think this evolution was based on principle—firms were finally seeing the light—but it was probably more because there just wasn't as much money to be made doing things the old way anymore. The stock market fell sharply, technology stocks declined by more than half, and as the hangover settled in, the country began to see some of the worst excesses of the prior few years, as companies like Enron and WorldCom blew up. Alan Greenspan railed against "infectious greed." The technology group at Credit Suisse faced a wave of negative publicity about its handling of tech deals, including a conviction (later overturned) for Frank Quattrone on charges of obstruction of justice. Credit Suisse would ultimately pay $200 million including penalties, fees, and other charges related to the SEC and state attorney general investigations into its handling of new stocks.

More gratifying to me was that the conflicts of interest among analysts were starting to become public knowledge. As analysts maintained buy ratings on tech stocks that were plummeting in value, investors began to realize that a lot of those analysts weren't doing anything close to objective research for their clients. Eliot Spitzer, who was then serving as New York State attorney general, did some investigating in conjunction with the SEC and identified the worst offenders.

Citigroup was among them—the company had a telecom analyst in the 1990s named Jack Grubman. He worked at Salomon Smith Barney, which was bought by Citigroup in 1998, the same year that Citi merged with Travelers; those deals formed the bulk of what is Citi today. Grubman was incredibly powerful during the tech bubble, yet he did cartwheels across the line that divides analysts from investment bankers. Grubman advised companies on deals, gaining access to critical information that would impact the stock price, and then wrote supposedly impartial research about those stocks. As he glibly put it, "What used to be a conflict is now a synergy."

Even worse, Grubman allegedly changed the rating on a stock in exchange for an unusual perk. In 1999, he upgraded AT&T as a personal favor from way up the executive food chain, and which he later boasted about in a widely publicized e-mail. The stock upgrade was allegedly parlayed into entrance for his young twins to a coveted private nursery school, via a good word from Sandy Weill, then Citigroup's CEO, who had directed $1 million in Citigroup donations to the school. This is something that could happen only in Manhattan. Grubman ended up paying a $15 million fine and was banned from the securities industry for life, but no criminal charges were ever filed, and he walked away with a $32 million severance package.

At Merrill Lynch, there were several others who flouted similar conflicts of interest. One tech analyst maintained unusually close ties with Tyco, one of the companies he covered. He sent CEO Dennis Kozlowski (who was later sent to prison for looting $100 million from the company) a $4,500 case of wine and sent the company's chief financial officer an advance copy of a report he was writing on Tyco, with a note saying "PLEASE REVIEW ASAP. I WILL NOT SEND OUT UNTIL I HEAR FROM YOU FIRST!" The analyst signed the note "LOYAL TYCO EMPLOYEE!" Henry Blodget, who followed tech stocks for Merrill Lynch, was fined $4 million and banned from the business for life. I considered it a compliment when one newspaper later described me as the "anti-Blodget."

Ultimately, ten of the biggest banks on Wall Street would settle the enforcement actions taken against them by Spitzer and the SEC. In addition to personal fines, those 10 banks paid $1.4 billion in fines in what was called the "Global Settlement," intended to address problems their analysts had caused. In addition, all banks on Wall Street had to put up a so-called Chinese wall between their equity research and investment banking divisions. That did a lot of good, and it thinned the ranks of analysts—a lot of people who couldn't or wouldn't do their own independent research had to find some other career.

In the midst of these investigations, I was asked to testify before the Senate Banking Committee about Wall Street analysts and the conflicts they face. I had a big spotlight on me and the arguments I had been making for nearly a decade on Wall Street. I worked and reworked my testimony in the days leading up to the hearings, which were covered prominently in that day's edition of the *Wall Street Journal*.

The testimony took place on March 19, 2002. Senator Paul Sarbanes, the chair of the committee, represented my home state of Maryland, and I figured he was a fan of the University of Maryland's basketball team. I began my testimony by saying that I hoped the University of Maryland team would go far that year and that I knew the chairman felt the same way. (As it turned out, they would win the national championship a few weeks later, the only time in the school's history.) Then I gave an analogy that seemed appropriate: Working as a truly objective analyst, I said, is like "playing basketball with one hand behind your back."

I cited numbers showing that the brokerage industry in 2002 earned four times as much from serving corporations, through investment banking and related services, than from serving investors. Two decades earlier, that ratio was about even, I said. "So who really is the client?"

In my conclusion, I summed up the role that independent analysts play in the financial system. "We have the best capital markets in the world," I said, "but let's not grade ourselves on a curve. They can be better. As analysts, we're at the intersection between the interests of corporations and the interests of investors. We provide institutional memory, act skeptically, challenge corporate authority, question assumptions, and speak up if something does not smell right. We are on the front lines of holding corporations accountable."

In the end, I felt great about the experience, as it seemed like a vindication of the arguments I'd been making for years—arguments that had cost me money and jobs and prestige. Those hearings would help form the basis of the Sarbanes-Oxley Act, which, among other things, requires CEOs to personally sign off on their companies' financial statements, so they could no longer plead total ignorance about problems below them that might later come out. I have a letter on my desk from Senator Sarbanes, thanking me for the role I played in that legislation.

Between that and my new role at Prudential—not to mention all the cheerleader analysts being forced out of the industry—this felt like the high point of my career thus far. I had been through hell because of my principles, yet I'd stayed true to them and ultimately been proven right.

However, I had been on Wall Street long enough by this point to know that this glow might prove short-lived. If I needed any evidence, I merely had to consider the morning I spoke to Senator Sarbanes and the rest of the Banking Committee. I was there with one of the lawyers from Prudential, and as we were walking in, he was approached by an executive from Credit Suisse, my old firm, who told him in an ominous tone, "We have the Mike Mayo file." In other words, he implied, I should be careful. They had information on me, and they were prepared to take action if they didn't like what I said that day.

The insiders were down, but they weren't out. And even though the tech bubble had been punctured, another one was starting to inflate—housing.

Chapter 4

The Professional Gets Personal

I ultimately spent six years at Prudential, longer than anywhere else in my career to date, but the first year was probably the most satisfying. In time, I would run into more of the usual problems: banks and investors actively trying to undermine me because they didn't like my ratings. I was still negative on the sector, and this was a tough stance to take at the time because bank stocks were on the rise. I thought that the reasoning behind my calls was as sound as ever, but the prices were moving in the opposite direction. In other words, I felt that I would be right in the long run, and the rest of the market was wrong in the short term.

Citigroup epitomized the situation. I have a long and complicated relationship with that bank. In this particular period I was the most negative analyst on the company, while the stock kept rising. This felt like a "short squeeze," and it's a painful experience. The feeling is as though you're expecting the tide to go out when it's actually coming in, and every minute the water gets a little higher. I thought my argument on Citi was solid: The company had a litany of regulatory and legal problems that reflected poorly on its strategy and culture and—worse—left it potentially exposed to financial settlements that would be required to make the problems go away. Those settlements ultimately would come to pass.

But even if my rationale was legitimate, the market wasn't buying it. For the next year, Citi's shares crept ever upward, from about $30 to $45 by mid-2003, and I was on the wrong side of that trend. The issue with my view in the short term was that debt markets were improving, which meant that loan quality was likely getting better, too. Interest rates were at historic lows, and the real estate problems that would later impact Citi, and just about every other bank on Wall Street, had yet to really develop.

During this time, Citi froze me out—I wasn't given access to the company's senior managers. The CFO told me, in a needling way, "Mike, the stock's going up. You've got to get this right." He made it seem as if the stock price was the sole determinant of whether a company was operating well or not.

Finally, I had to bite the bullet and upgrade my rating on Citi. I thought the improving debt markets would allow the company to maintain a better loan portfolio than I'd originally expected. I also crunched some numbers and thought that there was a good chance Citi would increase its dividend by a significant margin, possibly double digits, which would cause another big bump in the stock, and make my negative call even more vulnerable.

I had one more bit of evidence to add to the pile. In July 2003, I was having lunch with an investor at Bice, an Italian place in midtown Manhattan. Between bites of tartar di tonno, I saw the CFO of Citigroup walk in. He stopped at our table to say hello, then sat by himself and opened the *New York Post* to the sports section. In four working days, the company was going to announce earnings and review the dividend. This is usually the period when the finance department is scrambling to get everything done: reviewing press releases, rehearsing the earnings presentation. Yet the CFO was in here, casual and confident, eating a leisurely lunch by himself and reading about the Yankees. It was like a tell in poker—an action that reveals what someone's holding. I figured he had to have good news. A day or so later, I changed my rating from a sell to a hold, and at the company's quarterly earnings announcement, Citi increased its dividend by more than half, causing a short-term pop in the stock. It felt like a classic short squeeze, and my upgrade was akin to covering my position (and also my butt).

Much of this time in my career was like that. In part because of the call on Citi, my rankings dipped at Prudential. Analysts get judged on a variety of factors, including votes from clients and from the in-house salespeople that communicate our ratings to those firms. In the past, I'd always done well in those rankings, but in the third quarter of 2003, my internal scores were noticeably down. My boss was matter-of-fact about the situation. "It's a pure meritocracy," he said. In other words, there's no crying on Wall Street. The numbers are all that matter, and if your numbers aren't good, it really doesn't matter how legitimate your excuse might be.

■ ■ ■

In my mind, I *did* have a legitimate excuse. My stepdad—the man who more or less raised me—was in a serious car accident. In mid-April 2003, he called me from a hospital in Florida. He had been making a left-hand turn on a major road when another car ran into him. He had a collapsed lung, among other injuries, so he was having difficulty breathing. That would be the last time he would be able to speak with me.

I flew down immediately, and by the time I got there, he was in the intensive care unit, with a breathing tube. He was conscious, though, so we could write notes back and forth. It was a beautiful day, and I remember thinking how much he would have enjoyed going out for a round of golf, like we used to.

The hospital gave me a plastic bag with his wallet, keys, money, and a lottery ticket. I stayed at his place during that first trip down, assuming that he would get better, as he always had before. When I got to his apartment, I was happy to see that it was more like a bachelor pad than anything else: a half-made bed, a cigar in a full ashtray. His gun was in the drawer of his nightstand—the same gun he'd always kept within arm's reach when he slept. In the freezer was a half-full bottle of Absolut vodka and, in the refrigerator, kalamata olives. (His signature drink was vodka straight up, a couple of ice cubes, and an olive.) That made me smile. His doctors had told him to stop drinking and smoking, but he'd always lived life exactly the way he wanted to.

In his bedroom was a picture of him and my mother, dressed up for some black-tie event. Another photograph showed the words "Mike and Norma" traced in the sand. My mom and stepdad felt that other people always wanted their type of bliss in a relationship and that it was the lack of a love like this that made most people so petty.

Seven years before my stepdad's accident, in 1996, my mom had died at age fifty-nine from a recurrence of breast cancer. During her treatment, I'd adjusted my schedule to be with her in Washington as much as possible. In fact, my stepdad and I had gone through that experience together. I even went with him to the funeral home to pick out a casket. We told her we were just going out for a bit, but she knew. I could tell by the way she watched us leave. The man showed us a room filled with models—pine, poplar, oak, maple, walnut, cherry, mahogany, all with different stains and different designs. My stepdad said, "What's the difference? You get buried and no one sees you. Just give us the cheapest." When the man showed us a plain pine box, my stepdad said, "What? I wouldn't bury a dog in that." We settled on something more upscale.

On the day of her funeral, the hearse that was to take us all to the funeral home got lost on the way. My stepdad hated to ask for directions—when he got lost he used to say "They moved the road"—and we barely made it to her funeral on time. It was one last cosmic joke, and one that I think she would have enjoyed. After her death, my stepdad had been utterly lost for a little while, but once he started to get his bearings, he left Bethesda and moved to Pompano Beach, Florida. He'd been fine for a few years, and then in 2003, he had the car wreck.

Just as I'd done with my mother, I started juggling trips down to see my stepdad with other stops throughout the Southeast, meeting investors and bank executives whenever I could. This was during my short squeeze on Citi, and I distinctly remember sitting in a chair outside the intensive care unit at the hospital, checking CNBC and seeing that Citi was up a buck, up another buck . . . The pressure was tremendous, on both a personal and a professional level.

When I saw my stepdad a few weeks after the accident, he was dramatically worse. His leg was enormously swollen because of a blood clot, and he had trouble jotting notes down on a pad. Infections were ravaging his body. He laboriously communicated that his former girlfriend had some things he wanted me to collect, including his memoirs. I realized that he wouldn't be returning to his apartment, which meant I would need to pack the place up.

On my next visit, he was on a ventilator, sedated, and swollen almost beyond recognition. It seemed like it should have been a hard decision, but it really wasn't. I called my wife and also spoke with my two sisters, and everyone agreed: We would withdraw life support. He wouldn't have wanted to live that way. He had always told us that.

The following morning, the doctors removed his ventilator. Life is unlike the movies in so many ways, and this was one. Without the tube, he remained alive, medicated but breathing on his own. So I sat down to wait, alone. I had wondered what this experience might be like, but I hadn't pictured this scenario. When he died, I did the first thing that came to mind, which was to recite the Shema, the central prayer in the Jewish service. It's traditional for Jews to say the Shema as their last words, so I recited it for him. Back in New York and in front of our apartment building, I dropped my bags with the doorman and hurried to a nearby synagogue, where services were still taking place even though it was after 9:00 P.M. Not long after I sat down, the rabbi led the recitation of the Mourners' Kaddish, or the prayer to pay respect to the deceased. The rabbi asked if anyone wanted people included in the prayer, and I shouted out my stepdad's name.

He was buried in a plot next to my mother's, even in the same type of casket—the style he'd chosen for her years earlier. He was seventy-two and had lived every single day of his life the way he'd wanted. When I spoke at his funeral I emphasized this. Yes, he took chances. He drove a little recklessly, drank too much, smoked too much, but all with his eyes wide open. He always said he'd rather live well with risks than play it safe and be bored. That's something I've tried to apply to my own life and career, as well. With everything he'd done—escaping Romania, serving in the Israeli navy for a decade, smuggling black market goods, jumping ship from a merchant vessel to get to America, running businesses here—he was like the protagonist in a novel. I talked about this in my eulogy and summed up his life in two words: No regrets.

■ ■ ■

That didn't make it any easier at work, though. Besides Citi, my other calls were drawing the predictable backlash from investors and the banks themselves. When I'd initiated coverage at Prudential with nine sell ratings, I held a conference call to discuss my research, and I was on the receiving end of nasty comments about my position on Bank of New York. I got the distinct sense that people at the bank were feeding information to investors who, in turn, parroted the bank's argument.

In some rare cases, the attacks were face-to-face. These were equally unpleasant experiences, but at least I was in the room to defend myself. In one meeting with a large institutional money management firm, I sat down with the firm's own bank analyst, who repeatedly tried to bully me, insulting me and shouting over me whenever I spoke. I was at one end of the conference table and he was at the other, with a long line of his portfolio managers on both sides. For every argument I offered, he not only put forth a counterargument but added a personal attack, as well. When I said that I had done a 1,000-page research report, he said, "That's just a data dump. You didn't even do that work; your assistants did. You probably don't even know what's in that report." The meeting was so bad that I got a call afterward from someone in his firm who called to apologize and disassociate himself from the analyst.

After another meeting in New Jersey, one of the more senior portfolio managers offered to "advise" me about my views on the banking industry. The old-timer pulled me into a semidarkened room, just the two of us. "I've been doing this awhile," he said, "and you've gotta know when to change your view. You can't be so negative." He probably meant it as kindly advice from someone who had been around the block, but it came across more like a disciplinarian father scolding his son. His argument seemed to be that as long as the stock prices were going up, the banks' management and operating strategies didn't matter. After the tech bubble and collapse of a few years earlier, which showed how far stock prices can deviate from a company's fundamental performance, I thought that logic was fundamentally flawed.

Other companies limited my access to senior executives. Goldman Sachs was fairly up front about it, a rarity in the industry. I had recently initiated coverage on the firm, so I had few established relationships I could leverage. When I told one point of contact at the company that I'd like to have more meetings with management, he told me that the firm wasn't singling me out—they treated everyone that way. When I pushed a little harder for a meeting, I received a message that we needed to *have a conversation.*

Feeling like a student being reprimanded by a teacher, I was told that the most efficient use of management's time was for the executives to generate money for the firm instead of talking to the twenty or so analysts covering the company. An analyst like me would simply have to be patient. While I could live with this—to a degree—the gatekeeper added one more point: a consideration in granting analysts meetings with management of Goldman Sachs was the analyst's standing, influence, and knowledge. "In other words," the gatekeeper added, "we evaluate you." Here I was again—an outsider, trying to gain access to a place where some people didn't want me, solely so that I could do my job. It was like being back at the beginning of my first job search when Goldman sent me a letter effectively saying "Don't call us, we'll call you."

I thought Goldman's position was ironic—didn't I get any credit for my calls being accurate over the past decade? Wasn't I right about the rally in bank stocks during the second half of the 1990s and right about the negative direction of the sector starting in 1999? Had I not risked my career by going negative on the entire industry when I thought it was warranted? Moreover, in the aftermath of the "global settlement" that Eliot Spitzer and the SEC had hammered out with banks, and as the ranks continued to thin, I was one of the analysts who had stayed away from those issues, who had put the needs of clients first and tried to do my job the right way.

There were a couple of odd things about that settlement, however: It only punished the analysts, and the firms where they worked, for overly positive behavior. There wasn't any punishment—and there still isn't—for when companies try to retaliate against analysts who they think are overly negative. Companies can refuse to let you meet with management, ignore your questions during earnings calls, and more.

At times the backlash can be more insidious and subtle. Sometimes, as I would soon learn, it can be something as small as a joke.

■ ■ ■

In 2004, while still at Prudential, I had one of the most direct and personal conflicts of my career. It was with Jamie Dimon, the man who today runs all of JPMorgan Chase, making him one of the biggest power players on Wall Street. I'd had a cordial relationship with Dimon in the past. After he left Citigroup in 1998, I called to offer him my support and see if he would talk to me about the company when no executives there would. Similarly, after I was fired from Credit Suisse and he became head of Bank One, he called to wish me well and even mentioned a job possibility.

Despite this collegiality, I had a negative rating on Bank One, a position I'd maintained going back to 1999. The company had been a mess under John McCoy, and I felt there was simply too much left to clean up. In early 2004, Dimon arranged to sell the company to JPMorgan. It was a good deal for Bank One—the $58 billion price reflected a 10 percent premium to the company's current stock price— and for Dimon personally, as he would be CEO of the combined firm.

The deal presented a quandary for me, though. I already had a buy on JPMorgan, and in the limbo period between when a merger is announced and completed, the two stocks tend to move in tandem. So I upgraded the rating on Bank One to a buy, as well.

The next day, I made a point to arrive early at the presentation where the management of both companies would formally announce the merger and answer any questions. It was held at the Equitable Building in Midtown Manhattan on a snowy day. I fought through the storm and paid a gypsy cab quadruple the usual fare. The event was a significant milestone in both my world of banks and in corporate America as a whole. Dimon was like a dethroned king returning to claim his birthright. After being forced out by Sandy Weill at Citigroup, where he was the presumptive heir, and being effectively banished to run a smaller bank in Chicago, he was back. The JPMorgan deal was a major coup, and Dimon was coming home to New York at the top spot of what would be a direct rival to Citi, his old firm.

The room was packed, and there were hundreds of listeners on the conference lines—investors, colleagues, management at other banks, deal makers, press, regulators, and pretty much everyone else in my professional life. You often see press at merger announcements, but this one had TV cameras too. It was huge.

After a summary of the new firm, its strategy, and earnings expectations, Dimon opened the room up to questions. I raised my hand to ask a question—I can't even remember what it was about—and just as I handed the microphone back to the attendant, Dimon suckerpunched me.

"Mike Mayo," he said. "Ever since I came to Bank One he said to sell the stock . . . last night he upgraded the stock to 'buy.' . . . The title of his next report should be 'I Was Wrong.'"

My insides froze. The entire audience erupted in laughter. Not a little bit—they laughed uncontrollably. I saw someone to my left literally roll forward in his chair. In reality, this wave of laughter probably lasted a few seconds, but in that distorted way that time stops at emotional moments, it felt like hours. My peers, my clients, and the reporters—the people recording this event—were all laughing at me as if I were the kid in the school cafeteria who had dropped his tray of food.

I tried to say that this wasn't true—I had actually been right about Bank One. After all, I put a sell rating on the stock at $60 and it was currently at $45 (before the deal) or $50 (with the takeover premium). The microphone had been taken away from me, though, so I blurted this out to Dimon directly, barely above the noise of the crowd. His response was that I'd had a sell rating at a much lower price, too. In other words, I didn't call the company's rebound.

I could have come back by saying that his company had risen about in line with other large banks—that is, he hadn't done anything exceptional prior to the merger. Or that he'd possibly sold because of weak prospects at Bank One, which would cause him to fall short of the ambitious growth targets he'd set. But with almost no one in the room hearing anything I said—Dimon had a microphone; I didn't—I decided that this line of banter would not work. The dynamic was like a heckler trying to go against a comedian who had the rest of the crowd on his side.

One of the toughest things an analyst has to do is admit a mistake. If you're wrong only 45 percent of the time, you're one of the best.

One top investor told me that, during job interviews, he asks potential candidates how he or she handles mistakes. Similarly, analysts look at companies that make strategic errors to see how they'll respond. Are they chasing fads or actually learning from the mistakes to become better? My position on Bank One—part of the big call in 1999, when I'd gone negative on the entire banking sector—resulted in a net gain for the clients who had listened. Yet I could have called the bottom, put a buy on the stock, and done even better.

I'd had to make one very public admission of a mistake years earlier, when I'd predicted that a merger involving PNC would be voted down by shareholders. It wasn't; the merger went forward as planned, and I admitted as much in a research report: "I thought that shareholders would turn down the deal. I was wrong." I gave that same statement to the *Wall Street Journal*, an admission made easier because I was leaving for a business trip to Europe the next day; I knew I wouldn't have to immediately see or talk to anyone who'd read the story in the *Journal* and knew the entire saga. That had been a painful step and part of my learning process as an analyst.

A decade later, I found myself in that room at the Equitable Building in a similar situation. Jamie Dimon was at the podium, beaming. He had made investors money from the time he got to Bank One, and this was his victory lap. More than anything, I didn't want this situation to get away from me. The microphone was already gone, and there was a chance the next question would come soon. Doing nothing—leaving this unresolved—would be like leaving a piece of shrapnel in a wound instead of cleaning it out right away. I imagined the next few months as one long repetition of the question: "Are you going to write the report that Dimon asked for and call it 'I Was Wrong'?"

My decision seemed clear. I waved my hand for the audience microphone again. The attendant who passed it back to me had a smirk on his face, which I interpreted as the collective mood of the room. I stood up and said, "Jamie, it's Mike Mayo. Since you took over at Bank One, I was wrong." The audience let out a noise, like a dejected exhalation, and then went silent. The attendant handed the microphone to another person for the next question, and the meeting moved on. I sat immobile in my seat, staring straight ahead, not looking at anyone or anything. It was, without a doubt, the most humiliating moment of my career.

■ ■ ■

I would replay that incident over the next few years, usually with a shudder, thinking that I'd probably done the right thing but also that I'd been more or less forced into it. Then, two years later, another attack came. By then Dimon was firmly entrenched as the CEO of JPMorgan Chase, one of the largest banks in the world, with more than $1 trillion in assets. At a Citigroup financial services conference in late January 2006, he served as the keynote speaker.

It was a similar situation, with hundreds of people in the audience, including many of my most important clients. The event was for investors only, not analysts, and so I wasn't there. When Dimon took the podium, he began his speech by saying "This morning, someone gave me an analyst report by Mike Mayo, who I believe has had both JPMorgan Chase and Bank One on his sell list for probably ten or fifteen years, and this morning, he put us on his buy list. So I called him up. I said, 'You know what, first of all, I'd like to prove you right . . . you've been wrong for so long, I hope it's a good omen that you have us on your buy list."

When I heard the replay on JPMorgan's Web site, I was somewhere between astounded and infuriated, and for the next few hours, I paced in my office while I thought about the best way to respond. I would call the Fed, the SEC, Senator Sarbanes himself! I considered simply dropping the company from coverage and proposed that to my boss at Prudential. He said that Dimon might be happy to be rid of me and the kind of objective analysis I was known for. I then thought I should simply tell the investor relations person at JPMorgan to correct the situation. But this seemed wimpy—the equivalent of calling Daddy. After all, this situation gave me a second opportunity to rectify the embarrassment of two years earlier, but with a key difference.

Dimon had criticized my entire record on Bank One and JPMorgan Chase—not simply the stint since he had arrived—and I'd been right on the two companies during most of that longer period. After a day

and a half of working with my boss and our legal team, we drafted
a research note that I would release to clients and the press in which
I would take Dimon head-on. It read in part:

---

*As speakers often do, the CEO opened his remarks with a joke . . .
at my expense. Sell-side analysts who can't take a joke don't survive
very long, since our every move leaves a permanent record. With
the benefit of hindsight, some of these moves are, well, funny. Most
good jokes involve a lot of "rounding" of the facts to make a point,
and Mr. Dimon's was no exception. Those who may be unfamiliar
with his humor and with our work may not have recognized the
rounding in the joke, and that rounding was, I might add, enough
to put our highly vaunted sense of humor at risk.*

I included a table of my stock ratings of both Bank One and
JPMorgan Chase over the years, including the fact that I had a buy
on Bank One from 1994 to 1998, when the stock nearly tripled, and
a sell on JPMorgan from mid-2001 to mid-2002, when shares fell by
about a third.

The next morning, the *Financial Times* put a story about my report—
with my numbers—on the front page of the second section. Score. The
story talked about the pressures that analysts face if they say something
companies don't like. A little while later Dow Jones picked up the story.
I started to get a few e-mails from investors early that morning saying
"Way to go."

At 9:45 that morning, I was getting out of a cab on Park Avenue,
heading to a meeting with Jimmy Cayne, the head of Bear Stearns, when
my cell phone rang. It was my secretary, with the stunning news that
she had Jamie Dimon on the line. She patched his office through to me
and Dimon said that he didn't mean any harm with his comments. He'd
spoken of me out of respect, he said. It was a joke, nothing more.

"Maybe you meant it as a joke," I said, gathering myself, "but it
created a perception with hundreds of my most important investors

that I was a bad stock-picker. How is this going to be corrected?" I then asked if he could set the record straight in some public forum and also meet with me to talk about JPMorgan's current prospects.

He responded that he would meet with me and said that he agreed with the *Financial Times* article and had been too loose with the facts. That was it. End of call.

At my Bear Stearns meeting, the subject came up, of course. Cayne, puffing out smoke from his cigar, asked me, "What's this deal with Jamie Dimon? Everyone's talking about it." I told him what had happened and asked what he would have done in the same situation. Bear had a very rough-and-tumble corporate culture, and his answer reflected that. "I would make him pay, sue, shame him," Cayne said. "A man goes after you personally and he's wrong and the facts go against him . . . I know something about the Bible and when you insult a man in public . . ." His voice trailed off, and I understood his implication—in that situation, anything goes.

I never had to resort to that kind of Old Testament vengeance. An hour or so later I got a call from the Dow Jones reporter covering the story, who said he heard that Dimon had called me personally to apologize. I was confused for a moment—he never actually apologized—but then I understood. He'd done the next best thing, and JPMorgan was now getting the word out. Dimon had done what I'd done two years earlier. He was in a bad spot, an uncomfortable position, and he wanted to end it quickly.

In the end, I stood up to one of the most powerful people on Wall Street and came away with my dignity and my reputation intact. Dimon agreed to a meeting with me, and we've been on professional terms since then.

After the whole incident was over, I got an e-mail from a person I had never met before. "Your actions were strong but gentlemanly," he said. Even though I didn't know this man, his words were extremely gratifying, as that was the result I'd intended.

Chapter 5

The Crisis

After a few years, the financial situation at Prudential Securities started to become precarious. The company had wanted to establish a business model based on pure research and trading— no investment banking, no conflicts of interest to muddy the waters. That also meant no fees from those divisions, and operating without that income was a difficult balance, one that very few U.S. institutional research firms have been able to pull off. For the first few years, 2001 to 2003, everything was fabulous. We had thousands of retail brokers who worked with individual investors, in addition to an institutional sales force that dealt with major firms. But Prudential didn't have the heritage or culture to operate this way. It eventually sold off the retail brokerage, meaning we suddenly had fewer ways to distribute—and get paid for—the research that the analysts were doing.

I began to look around for a new position. Not long after, the CEO of Prudential—not the securities unit, where I worked, but the entire corporation—came to speak to our division. We were just a tiny slice of the company at that point, and a slice that was getting steadily smaller. I was so concerned about the company's commitment to our business that I asked the CEO what seemed to me like a reasonable question: Was he willing to commit more capital to the securities business? Some of the managers at the securities unit thought that question was overly hostile, and I paid for it at bonus time, receiving an amount that was substantially lower than what I'd been told to expect.

I kept interviewing—not because of the bonus hit but more because I was concerned about my employer's declining prospects. In the spring of 2007, I moved my team to Deutsche Bank, and three months later, the parent company closed the securities unit for good. The *Wall Street Journal* ran a story about its demise, with a multidecade timeline, and my departure actually made the timeline. "Mike Mayo quits" was the very last item before the firm was shuttered.

Deutsche Bank was in downtown Manhattan, just a few blocks away from Prudential. It's the only major "Wall Street" bank that is actually located on Wall Street. As with my previous job changes, most everyone on my team came with me, in some cases people who had been working with me for nearly a decade. The new company had a stricter dress code, so the junior people had to buy some suits. Deutsche Bank had gone without bank analysts for several years, and we were eager to hit the ground running. My first report for the firm came out on April 25, 2007, within a month of when we started, and among traditional U.S. banks, it included exactly zero buys and sixteen sell or hold ratings.

We had access to fantastic resources at the firm. Deutsche Bank had a massive fixed-income division, far bigger than that at most other banks, with a lot of researchers and economists to support that business. A lot of people don't know this, but the bond market is orders of magnitude larger than the equities market—it's just massive, and it drives the national and global economies in major ways. On my second day, I walked upstairs and introduced myself to Deutsche Bank's chief economist, Peter Hooper, who had been one of the Federal Reserve's chief economists for many years. He had an insightful mind and maintained close relationships to Greenspan, yet he was very down to earth.

We would need those resources, though, because Deutsche Bank was also where I would experience the financial crisis, the biggest disruption in the banking sector—and the overall U.S. economy—since the Great Depression. The crisis has inspired a lot of soul searching among regulators, politicians, ratings agencies, homeowners, and investors. I'm not sure it's inspired enough soul searching among banks though. The fundamental question: How could this have happened?

The answer is that while some people knew things weren't right—and other people like me had been pounding the table since 1999—it was extremely difficult to see precisely how and when it would all blow up. If I had left equity research to launch a hedge fund and had to actually buy and sell stocks based on my opinions of the banking industry before the crisis hit, at times, I would have made investors a lot of money, but I probably would have folded several times as well.

The issue was not because of some flaw in my reasoning. I was right about the problems in banking—the outsized bets on real estate, the crony capitalism, the ridiculously excessive compensation that rewarded bank execs for taking on massive risks and didn't punish them for being wrong. No, my problem was that I was simply too early. There's a line that gets thrown around on Wall Street about situations like this: *The market can stay irrational longer than you can stay solvent.*

As with all irrational markets, you could make money by pretending that everything was fine. For a while, everything actually did look calm, for reasons that only became clear in hindsight. For one thing, the credit scores of a lot of people were actually going up during the mid-2000s. Why? Interest rates were abnormally low for so long that huge numbers of homeowners were refinancing their mortgages. From 2000 to 2007, more than half of the subprime mortgages were so-called cash-out refinancings, which involve paying off existing debt with cheaper new debt. Falling rates allowed borrowers to give themselves a raise by lowering their monthly payment, and rising real estate prices allowed them to give themselves a bonus by borrowing more against their home.

Only about a third of the mortgages originated during this period were to purchase a home. People used that cash for a variety of things—they redid their kitchens, took vacations, bought cars. Some people used the money to pay down their credit card bills, but a lot of it went to discretionary spending. The refinancings allowed them to pay cash for things they wanted rather than putting these purchases on a credit card or taking out another consumer loan with much higher interest rates than a mortgage. Why get a car loan at 8 percent when you can get a tax-deductible home equity loan at 5 percent? Debt is illusory, because it produces the appearance of having more money than you really have, but in this case it played tricks on credit scores, too.

This situation also meant that people were effectively doubling down on a bet that housing prices would not drop. Real estate had not declined nationwide since the Great Depression, and people figured that this was a precedent that would always hold since there were few people alive who remembered national home prices declining. With more being owed overall on houses, even if payments were smaller, borrowers had a much smaller margin of error before going underwater on their mortgage. In 2010, Jamie Dimon summed up the issue for the industry: "We never thought that housing prices would go down."

The second confusing element of the precrisis period was that the country's bankruptcy laws were revamped in late 2005. The new rules were much stricter and made it harder for bankrupt people to simply walk away from their debts. In the months leading up to that point, everyone who was even considering bankruptcy figured they should do it now, while the rules were still in their favor. They were playing beat the clock. That had the effect of emptying out the pipeline—you had a giant cluster of people filing for personal bankruptcy in late 2005, and for a while in 2006, there were very low filing rates. Even a year later, once the numbers started to pick up, the picture wasn't clear. As we entered 2007, it was hard to tell how much of the increases in bankruptcies and consumer loan losses were simply rebounds from the artificially low period and how much was a blinking red danger sign.

A third important aspect of this period was that banks were making record profits. For 2006 and the first half of 2007, U.S. banks collectively earned around $36 billion a quarter, which far exceeded the $26 billion a quarter they had averaged from 2001 through 2005 and was almost twice the profits they earned a decade earlier. At the same time, their "loan losses"—the amount they had to write off on bad debt—was close to an all-time low. The lack of loan losses seemed to indicate to a lot of people that any problems in the real estate market would be contained to the subprime loans. At the time, most bank analysts, including me, didn't think that subprime was a major factor on Wall Street. We knew about it but had no way of knowing it was such a large part of the banking system.

There were hordes of mortgage "originators," slimy operations like Countrywide, New Century, or Long Beach—none of which I covered, and none of which is around anymore—providing loans to questionable borrowers. These firms were growing by leaps and bounds, generating huge fees by persuading people to take loans they couldn't afford to pay off and then selling off those loans before the ink was dry. They were a dark corner of U.S. finance, and I thought they had little to do with Wall Street. But big U.S. banks were buying the loans created by these shady operations, packaging the debt into mortgage-backed securities and quickly off-loading them, we thought, to ill-informed institutional investors like European insurance companies. At least, that was the thinking. It simply didn't occur to me that banks actually owned this toxic debt for any meaningful length of time, leaving them seriously exposed. The common refrain back then was that banks were in the "moving business, not the storage business." Worse, they owned it in hard-to-find corners of their balance sheets, like investment banking trading assets and commitments. It wasn't transparent at all, sometimes not even to senior management within the banks.

While subprime loans in the United States were only about 10 percent of all mortgage loans, what we and the banks didn't understand was that once the subprime borrowers were ridden for all they were worth and eliminated from the market, the effects would be far reaching. When people don't intend to pay back money they're borrowing, they tend to spend that money recklessly, and that was certainly the case in housing. Subprime borrowers were willing to bid up home prices because they assumed that they would either be able to flip the house for a profit or refinance into a cheaper loan at some point in the future.

In mid-2007, though, the problems started showing up. Home prices in the highest-flying markets, such as Arizona, California, and Florida stopped going up, and many subprime borrowers were unable to repay their loans. In June of that year, Bear Stearns announced that it was pledging $3.2 billion in loans to two of its in-house hedge funds, because of subprime losses and investor redemptions. A month later, the firm would tell investors that the funds had "very little" or "effectively no value" for investors, and by August, those two funds would file for bankruptcy; a third would have its assets frozen.

The big ratings agencies—Moody's and S&P, which had so gleefully assigned investment-grade ratings to mortgage-backed securities and related products (such as collateralized debt obligations [CDOs], which are funds in which the risk is divided up into pieces)—began to see rising defaults in the mortgages that made up those products. In the middle of 2007, they downgraded a bunch of them and took away their investment-grade rating—including some securities they'd originally evaluated less than twelve months earlier. That meant the institutional investors like pension funds and insurance companies, which were restricted to owning only investment-grade securities, could no longer hold them, not to mention buy new ones.

In the span of a couple of months, everyone was suddenly unloading this trash, no one wanted to buy it anymore, and the pipeline of new deals completely seized up. Banks that had been securitizing mortgage-backed bonds in high volumes were left holding them and their underlying mortgages, tens of billions' worth, though that information hadn't come out yet. This was like the period when Wile E. Coyote runs off the canyon wall but hasn't fallen yet. It was only a matter of time.

■ ■ ■

For me, the real start of the crisis came on the night of October 11, 2007. I was at Madison Square Garden with my son, watching the New York Knicks play a preseason exhibition game against Maccabi, a pro basketball team from Tel Aviv. This is an annual event, and it's a big deal to a lot of the Jewish population in New York. People chant and sing the Hatikvah, the Israeli national anthem. Even for a Reform Jew like me, it's an experience.

Late in the first half, I got a call from a *New York Times* reporter. "You see this stuff coming over on Citi?" he said. I'd actually been absorbed in the game and enjoying time with my son, and had not checked my BlackBerry that night, so I wasn't sure what he was talking about. The reporter told me that Chuck Prince, the CEO of Citigroup, had restructured the company, yet again, merging some units and firing some very senior executives. "What about Prince himself?" I asked. My thinking was that if he left, that would be good news. If not, the company's problems weren't going away, no matter how many people he fired. The reporter said no, Prince was staying around.

This was outrageous. Chuck Prince should never have been in the top spot at Citi in the first place. He had served as general counsel for two decades, aside from short stints in an operating role. This was completely different from most CEOs, who work their way up through the ranks by running successful business lines of increasing size and scope. Prince seemed to get the job primarily because he was a confidant and trusted aide of the former CEO, Sandy Weill, a role in which he had helped the company navigate its many regulatory crises. When I mentioned Chuck Prince to investors, they'd say "Oh, the lawyer."

He started as CEO in October 2003, and even early on his statements contradicted each other. He stressed the need for better controls while also pursuing aggressive growth—two goals that are diametrically opposed. Just one year into the job, Citi already was falling short of expectations. Expenses started to grow faster than revenues, Citi backpedaled on prior targets, and several managers left. After two years, Citigroup's stock had gone nowhere, while an index of similar companies had increased 44 percent. Going into 2007, Prince said it would be the "Year of No Excuses," but the company continued to underperform in terms of profits, stock price, or just about any other measure you looked at.

The job seemed to take a physical toll on Prince—he looked tired and haggard when I saw him in person. In June 2007, he gave a notorious quote to the *Financial Times* about how the company was still providing credit for leveraged buyouts. "When the music stops, in terms of liquidity, things will be complicated," he said. "But as long as the music is playing, you've got to get up and dance. We're still dancing."

He seemed to be saying that he knew these loans were getting dicey, but he had to keep making them, simply because everyone else was. During the Financial Crisis Inquiry Commission hearings in 2010, Prince would later try to explain the context of this quote, saying that he knew loose credit was a problem but that he had to maintain the relaxed standards in order to attract leveraged-buyout deal makers. He also told the astonished commission members that he had even asked for greater regulation. In other words, he asked the government to compel his company to do the right thing, like a drug addict hoping to get caught and forced into rehab.

When the reporter called, however, Prince was still at the top of Citi after four years of poor performance, and I was in my seat at Madison Square Garden, watching the Knicks beat up on the Israeli team. As soon as I got off the phone, I scrambled the jets. One of my senior staffers, Tom, was actually still at the office, so I called and told him to start working on a report about the news. My son and I left the game at halftime. The Israeli basketball team would have to wait. We got home around 9:30, and I started working from my home office, coordinating with Tom over the phone.

It was about to get worse. Around 11:00 that night, online news stories of the management shakeup started appearing, and they quoted Robert Rubin, chair of Citi's executive committee and the former Treasury Secretary in the Clinton Administration. Rubin praised Prince and said that he would be around "for many years to come." I'm sure he meant this as a way to boost the market's confidence in the CEO and the company as a whole—after all, this was Bob Rubin!—but to my mind it had the exact opposite effect. I thought his public support of Prince amounted to one of two things: either an utter disdain for the company's shareholders, or a sign that Rubin was seriously, almost pathologically, out of touch regarding the problems plaguing Citi. Of those two options, I wasn't sure which was worse.

Before Rubin's statement, I was ready to downgrade the stock from a buy to a hold, but after I saw that, I went all the way to sell. That's extremely rare—it's like going sixty miles per hour, slamming on the brakes, and putting the car in reverse —but I had seen enough. Prince and the other managers had missed their targets, and they had the wrong targets anyway. I had done my homework.

That night I probably got about two hours of sleep, and Tom got none. He ended up staying at the office for thirty-six straight hours, even though his apartment was literally across the street from our office. The report was done by midnight or so, but because this was going to be a controversial call, Deutsche Bank insisted that we get it approved by multiple levels of management, including senior executives in Germany. After bouncing the report across the Atlantic a few times, we ended up scaling back the language in several key spots, but the overall conclusions remained the same, and the report went out first thing in the morning.

I went on the air on CNBC that day for the first time in four years to explain the call, saying that we had huge concerns about the lack of execution of plans and the lack of corporate governance at Citi. I also said that while Prince had called 2007 the "Year of No Excuses," it was looking more to us like the "Year of No Repercussions." (In fact, that theme seems to have continued for Citi even after the crisis.) I said Prince should be fired and added that Rubin—whom the CNBC commentator called a "mythical character in American financial management"—was not accountable and therefore did not justify his huge Citi salary, which would total $100 million by the end of the decade. "We have not heard from one investor who's ever spoken with Robert Rubin," I said.

This was approaching sacrilege. Rubin really was a legendary figure—the boy wonder who had begun his career on Wall Street in the 1960s and rose to become co-CEO of Goldman Sachs. He later ran the Treasury Department in the Clinton Administration from 1995 to 1999, where he helped defuse the Mexican financial crisis and oversaw an unprecedented period of stability and expansion in the U.S. economy. He was that rare figure who succeeded at the highest levels in both the private and public sector. But at Citi he was more like an *éminence grise*, with no operational responsibilities.

A few days after my downgrade, Citi announced its third-quarter earnings, and they were certifiably horrific: Earnings were down 60 percent, largely due to write-downs for securities backed by subprime mortgages and to corporate loans related to leveraged buyouts. The music had stopped; Citi was no longer dancing. Prince did not do himself any favors on the earnings call when he labeled the results "frankly surprising." During the Q&A segment, I flat-out asked if he should keep his position: "You guys say the results are disappointing. So what are the repercussions at the level of the office of the chairman?" Prince dodged the question, and my exchange with him was actually covered in the press, which I found somewhat mystifying. I was simply verbalizing what everyone else on the call—and everyone else in the business world—was thinking.

A few days later, Prince was gone, taking a $38 million severance package with him. This included allowing him to keep $28 million in unvested compensation—i.e., previously announced bonuses that were not yet paid—plus a $10 million bonus for 2007. Given that Citi needed to get rid of Prince quickly, allowing him to keep his restricted compensation made some sense, even if it seemed distasteful. However, giving him a $10 million bonus for 2007, a year in which he was seemingly forced to leave due to mismanagement, is shameful. In total, Prince earned $110 million in total compensation while he was CEO at Citigroup.

This is one of the key reasons why things haven't changed on Wall Street. Few of the people who got us into the crisis were punished for their actions. In most cases, they were rewarded. They lost their title and their responsibility, but they were ushered out the door with eight-figure packages.

When I downgraded to a sell rating, Citi's shares were trading at $48, but two months later they were below $30. And they just kept sliding, all the way to the single digits, where they would continue to languish for years. (Eventually, the company reverse-split its shares at 10 to 1, which made a lousy $4 stock into a $40 stock.) By late 2007, the problems that Citi experienced were starting to show up at other companies, too.

■ ■ ■

Within a few weeks of the Citi downgrade, I had a similar exchange with Stan O'Neal, then CEO of Merrill Lynch. The company announced its own third-quarter 2007 numbers, and they were pretty horrendous because of the toxic securities it owned, almost all backed by dodgy mortgages. As a result, the company would actually lose money for the quarter.

Compounding the matter, Merrill had shown signs of being slippery with its disclosures in the past. Earlier that year, in April 2007, the company had said during its first-quarter earnings call that its U.S. subprime mortgage activities were less than 1 percent of total revenues for the firm over the prior 15 months. This was the dark-corner theory of subprime—*yes, the stuff is bad, but we don't have very much of it.*

The flaw in that logic was that Merrill was talking about revenue, and we needed to know about the firm's risk exposure. It's like saying "We don't make very much money from selling dynamite" and neglecting to mention that you're sitting on a warehouse full of it.

The simple question during that call could have been: "What's the total amount of exposure in your firm from subprime securities?" That was a collective miss from everyone who covered the company, including me. But when October rolled around, and the company preannounced losses of $4.5 billion, only to increase that amount three weeks later to $8 billion, I had seen enough.

The company's financials were sufficiently complex that I knew there was no way anyone on the outside could figure out the actual exposure or what it meant. So why not just ask the people running the company? This time, I went straight to the CEO. It's a lesson I had learned over the years— on these calls, if you ask a question of someone farther down on the corporate ladder and the answer turns out to be wrong, executives will just throw that person under the bus. "He didn't know what he was talking about," they'll say. "*We* weren't wrong. *He* was." But when you ask the chief executive, there's no one for him to hide behind. Besides, who should know this information better than the company's CEO? Who's ultimately responsible?

So when I finally got to ask a question on that October 2007 call, I asked Stan O'Neal flat out what he thought about the company's situation. "Stan," I said, "do you feel comfortable that there's not another shoe to drop and a lot more write-downs on the [bad securities]?" O'Neal said no, he thought everything was fine—but he was wrong. The value of these assets was still declining, even as O'Neal refused to disclose the firm's total exposure, leaving many of us to believe that he didn't have his arms around the situation. Six days later, O'Neal was fired by Merrill's board on October 30, 2007.

After this, I developed a reputation as a CEO killer. Google searches of my name would pull up stories about Stan O'Neal. I didn't deliberately try to get him fired. Instead, I really just wanted to know the extent of Merrill's losses, and I believe he honestly didn't know when he answered my question. Yet the situation on Wall Street started to deteriorate fast. With each new disclosure by a big bank, the overall industry looked worse.

A few banks fessed up, though. The industry holds a big conference in Boston each fall, and at the event in November 2007, JPMorgan and Wells Fargo both admitted that they had some of the more toxic housing-related loans on their books. Earlier in the year, both had acquired a lot of brokered home equity loans, which are loans they had bought but not originated themselves. They admitted that the quality of these loans was pretty dubious; this was apparent almost from the day the loans were signed, given that some borrowers never made a single payment on them.

My team and I were still trying to figure out the kind of quality issues these banks might really face, but we knew that JPMorgan and Wells Fargo had both been fairly conservative with their growth strategies during the mid-2000s. Neither had purchased an "originator," which included the sketchy firms that generated fees by doing high-volume loans, often in the subprime category. In contrast, Lehman Brothers had found these fees—and the pipeline of mortgages that it could bundle into securities—sufficiently attractive that it purchased its own originator in 2004. This is akin to a seafood store deciding that it no longer wants to buy fish wholesale but would rather just purchase a boat and catch its own. Merrill Lynch, Morgan Stanley, and Bear Stearns all followed suit by buying their own originators.

But if relatively cautious and well-managed banks like JPMorgan and Wells were getting infected, others were likely to have even bigger problems, ones that they weren't willing to talk about yet. The challenge was how to figure out how big those problems might be. If you go back in history, losses on home equity debt typically average 0.3 percent, and the prior peak—the worst ever—was 0.48 percent in 1993. That's for a specific fiscal quarter, meaning that for every $100 the bank had loaned out, it would lose nearly $0.50.

In the midst of the crisis, my team started putting together models that said even if you double that and say it might be twice as bad as the *worst-ever* period in modern economic history, you set losses at 1 percent and figure you'll be OK. Except the losses ended up at more than 3 percent. To a person outside the banking industry, that doesn't sound particularly high, but it's off the charts: about six times the previous high. Think about it this way—the record for RBIs in a Major League Baseball season is 191. If someone was to have a fantastic season, he might someday beat that record. It's been in place since the 1930s. He might hit 195 RBIs, he might even break 200. But the idea that someone could hit more than 1,200 RBIs is basically unfathomable. This is what happened in the financial crisis.

That's why the challenge of the whole period wasn't merely to see that something was wrong. It was to realize exactly *how* wrong. I was an outlier in the industry—many people thought things were fine, and I knew they weren't—but I didn't know how bad they truly were. And once things started to turn, I was scrambling to keep up with the pace of developments. Even a hardened cynic like me, someone who's come to expect the worst behavior from banks, was stunned when the true extent of the situation became clear.

■　■　■

Shortly after Chuck Prince and Stan O'Neal got the ax, in November 2007, I went on CNBC again to air my concerns. I said the total cost of the crisis could approach $400 billion, a number that was much higher than anyone else's estimate to that point—and one that still turned out to be too low.

I came up with this figure by combining losses not only from banks but from everywhere else in the financial system, as well, including mortgages and related securities. The project had been difficult and tedious, and members of my team had stayed at the office until midnight each night for weeks to dig up data. Even with all that work, the $400 billion number was an estimate, but I figured that an imperfect estimate would be better than being perfectly wrong and waiting for the situation to clarify. At least I could be more vocal about my stance and help investors pull their money while the stock market—and the shares of most Wall Street banks—had yet to reflect these issues.

I also said that the banking industry had to come clean about the extent of its exposure to problem mortgages and other assets, and I compared the "everything's fine" approach thus far to the denials banks and thrifts had made during the savings and loan crisis. After eight years of warning about an impending storm, I was now shouting from the mountaintop, saying that it was time to take cover.

I also put my money where my mouth was, selling off all stocks in my personal portfolio and keeping my assets entirely in cash. That move was so conservative and unorthodox that my bank contacted me to make sure I really wanted to take such a step.

Those critical calls certainly got some attention, some of it favorable. While most people thought I was being alarmist, a few agreed with my thinking. Around this time, in late 2007, a sales rep at Deutsche Bank told me that one of her clients, a small, then-unknown hedge fund called Paulson & Co., wanted to meet with me. She called me again and again, and each time I told her that I didn't have time to meet with this person. Finally, she said, "It's all he wants for his birthday." I met with John Paulson, the manager of the fund, and gave him my thoughts on the banking sector. We had a pleasant discussion, and while he was very impressive, I didn't think much more about it.

A few weeks later, he called me, directly this time, and said he'd like to hire me. I've always been an equity analyst on the sell side, never working for hedge funds or money managers, and I wasn't sure I wanted to start now. "It would be very lucrative," he said, perhaps the understatement of the century. Still, I decided to stay the course. I was in the middle of a major crisis in my industry, and I felt like I was doing valuable work. Paulson would soon become almost unimaginably wealthy—he personally made $3.7 billion in 2007, and his firm made $15 billion because of favorable trades against mortgage-backed securities. If I had taken that job, my life would have changed in many ways, but I don't regret my decision.

Some of the attention my calls generated was less positive, however, even within my own firm. My supervisors at Deutsche Bank told me that I should avoid making those kinds of strong, negative comments about the banking sector in the press. I thought this was the same kind of institutional resistance I'd run into in the past, but not long after, I was summoned to a meeting on an upper floor of the building, where I had never been before, with the head of risk management for all of Deutsche Bank, the entire firm. He told me that the firm did not like to be seen as publicly negative on the U.S. banking sector at a time when it held certain short positions.

I didn't know what he was talking about and wouldn't piece it all together until later, when it came out that Deutsche Bank had made

$1.5 billion on one of its proprietary trades during the crisis by betting against mortgage-backed securities. The firm ended up losing about $4.5 billion overall, far less than most big banks, in part because of its aggressive short positions on the U.S. housing market. All I understood at the time was that I was now in a cone of silence. The bank wouldn't interfere with my analysis of the sector—I could still rate the banks however I saw fit, and I still had wide latitude to say whatever I wanted in my research reports—but I was under a gag rule when it came to any more media spots.

In the few months prior, I'd sounded the alarm, played a role in the firing of two bank CEOs, raised awareness of the rapidly spreading crisis, and was becoming a source for CNBC and a few other media outlets about the rapidly changing fortunes of the banking sector. Yet now I was locked in the closet again. This mattered. Banks and their insulated managements will pay attention to criticism from analysts like me, but only to a point. They have much more control over that information flow than when criticism makes it into the press. I could no longer talk to the broader financial community or to investors at large, only to institutional investors who were clients, and as a result, banks could more easily downplay their problems. I have no doubt that the crisis would have been substantially mitigated—in both duration and severity—if the true exposure to risky mortgages had come out sooner.

Chapter 6

The Vortex

For the rest of 2007 and early 2008, I struggled to keep up with developments in the sector. I started waking up in the middle of the night more frequently, when I would check the movement in overseas stocks or jot down some thoughts, and then try unsuccessfully to go back to sleep. My exercise routine went into overdrive, and even I recognized that it was starting to get ridiculous on some mornings. But it was a major stress release. I would do push-ups until I could do 100 at a time, then 200. I did this until I developed neck problems and had to shift to other exercises. I even tried to improve my diet, eating beets, spinach, egg whites, and other so-called superfoods. For a special treat, I would have chocolate tofu pudding for dessert.

It became harder and harder to make sense of the banks' prospects. Their operations were suddenly far more complex, and the market was extremely unstable. The traders in Deutsche Bank's big bond division became leading indicators. They were trading financial instruments called credit-default swaps (CDSs), which functioned as bets on whether a company would be able to survive. I cultivated relationships among those groups, asking for the CDS spread on Citi, or Bank of America, or Morgan Stanley. It felt like asking a Magic Eight Ball to explain the market.

Many of us had not dealt much with CDSs in the past, but during the crisis they became a new focus. These swaps act as insurance for the owners of debt. A company that owns a bond can buy a CDS contract, which requires that it pays a percentage, usually at least half a percent per year of the bond's value. In exchange, the company gets peace of mind: If the issuer defaults, the bondholder gets paid in full. The price of this protection "floats," depending on market sentiment. If a company seems to be in trouble, the CDS contracts start to cost more.

This component of analysis had little in common with my work in the past, either at the Fed or at my other jobs on Wall Street, or even with things I learned in business school or studying for the CFA exams. I had been trained to look at a company's fundamental performance— its business operations—rather than tracking the day-to-day movements of its stock. That was for traders focused on short-term gains, and it was a good way to lose money if you didn't have fighter-pilot nerves and a lot of experience.

We were looking to the market for answers on how stocks would react, and at times like that, when there's a lot of fear and uncertainty swirling around, the market can act in nonsensical ways. When rumors started to spread about a particular company during this period, CNBC would put its ticker at the top of the screen in bright orange, to show that the company was being actively monitored that day. If a bank showed up in orange, investors would start calling to ask what was going on. Some of them would shoot first—that is, sell the stock—and ask questions later. This alone drove stock prices down, leading to wider CDS spreads . . . and more calls and questions directed at me.

The market was behaving as a collective systematized momentum trader, reacting less to long-term prospects than to short-term price trends. The result was a self-fulfilling prophecy that caused extreme price swings and downward spirals in certain stocks, which I called "getting sucked into the vortex." When that happened, the difference between getting out of a stock on a Tuesday compared to a Wednesday could mean my clients might lose half of their position, with daily price swings that were a hundred times greater than average, representing years of performance under normal circumstances.

Bear Stearns was the first company to get sucked into the vortex. I had followed the stock but hadn't recommended it to clients, ever. Even under normal market conditions, there were simply too many unknown risks for me to feel comfortable with its operating model. Its two failed hedge funds were one of the earliest signs of trouble, leading to questions about further risks that the company could never really shed.

Subsequent signs appeared during a conference that I coordinated on March 15, 2008. It was a big event, with speakers like Alan Greenspan, the CEO of Deutsche Bank, and several housing experts. The conference featured a debate between hedge fund manager Steve Eisman and legendary investor Bill Miller of Legg Mason. Miller was asked about the rapidly declining share price of Bear Stearns, and he responded that he thought the stock presented good value. He had no way of knowing that the stock was down significantly that day, nor could he, or anyone, have predicted that the company was just days from going under. But Miller held his own, the conference was a success, and I celebrated with a previously planned family vacation to California. Little did I expect that Bear would go down during my vacation, just two days later.

We had booked a week at a small hotel in Santa Monica, where we would spend time with my sister and her kids. During that infamous Sunday, March 17, when everything was unfolding—regulators were swarming the headquarters of Bear, along with deal makers and due diligence people from JPMorgan, which ultimately bought Bear, and with teams from other banks that kicked the tires but decided not to buy— I was actually an hour south of Los Angeles, watching the worst Beatles tribute band ever. The concert was my idea, and I encouraged (my wife would probably use the term "forced") everyone to attend. The singer had an accent never heard from any Beatle, and our family made up more than half of the twenty or so people in the crowd, in a crumbling, decrepit concert hall. Before the show started, reporters were calling, telling me about the situation unfolding 2,800 miles away. I felt utterly, almost ludicrously out of the loop, but there was probably little I could do from there anyway, at least for the next hour or so.

After the show, I spent the drive back to Santa Monica franti-
cally making calls and trying to figure out how the increasingly likely
demise of Bear would impact the rest of the industry. Our hipster hotel
was uncomfortably stylish and not at all set up for children; our youngest daughter, two years old, kept wandering toward either the pool or
the fire pit. I was on the phone with my team talking about how a
Wall Street institution was crumbling while trying to do my part to
keep my toddler occupied and help find some kid-appropriate food.
All the while I wondered whether I should cut the vacation short and
return to New York. I knew that my wife would take a dim view of
having me go home, leaving her alone with our three young children.
To her, very little that happens on Wall Street justifies time away from
your family. So I stayed.

I worked all night that Sunday at the tiny "business center" next
to the front desk of the hotel. The time difference meant that I had a
few more hours on Sunday to process the events in New York, but it
also meant that I'd get no sleep that night. I finished my report though
and made it onto the Monday morning call 4:30 A.M. Pacific time with
the sales force to discuss what had happened. Over the next few days
I would struggle, trying to keep pace with events back in New York
while attempting to be part of the family vacation. We were at the beach
a lot, and maybe the perspective was healthy. Life goes on. Family mat-
ters more than a job.

Unfortunately, a few months later, when Lehman Brothers went
under—rather than being bought out for a fire-sale price like Bear—
I didn't have that perspective. I was all too close.

■ ■ ■

Lehman was by far the worst call of my career. I had recommended the
company to investors close to its peak in the spring of 2007, and even
after problems started showing up within the firm, I kept the company
at a buy. Primarily, my rating was on the basis of its book value. This
is the simplest version of a company's worth, defined as assets minus liabilities. It's what you'd be left with if you sold the company. In this
case, I made one major adjustment, scaling down its book value based
on the estimated losses on its real estate loans, which included unrealized losses on both residential and commercial real estate properties,

loans, and securities. The real estate guys at Deutsche Bank gave me worst-case scenarios for those holdings, and the result was that the stock traded at well more than one fourth below core book value, even factoring in these potential losses. Under normal circumstances, anything trading this far below core book value is an automatic "buy" rating. It's usually easy money, like finding a way to purchase dollar bills for 75 cents.

The research director tried several times to talk me into down-grading—he thought that the fear in the market was enough to over-come any kind of fundamental analysis like this. I held firm on my buy rating, and I was wrong. The CDS spreads on Lehman were widening rapidly—yawning open like fault lines in an earthquake movie—and the company still had no credible explanation for how it planned to deal with its real estate exposure. Hedge funds were steadily pulling business from Lehman throughout 2008, and by September of that year, it was starting to have a problem financing its daily operations.

On September 10, 2008, I had a slightly surreal exchange with Lehman's management during the quarterly earnings call. Lehman ann-ounced that it would lose $3.9 billion for the quarter, its biggest loss ever, and also that it was looking at selling off pieces of itself or the entire firm. On the off chance it could not find a buyer, Lehman had also proposed a Hail Mary play: It would take all its bad real estate debts, both commercial and residential, and spin them off into a new company. The plan was probably doomed from the start. Among other issues, that debt wouldn't be marked down. Instead, it would remain at whatever value the company wanted. Lehman was stuck in a corner on this—much of the debt was nearly worthless, given that there were no buyers for it—yet the company couldn't come right out and say this. As long as the numbers weren't real, no one would believe them, and the assets themselves would continue to rot.

An even bigger problem was that Lehman would require capital to fund the new spin-off structure, about $7 billion by its own estima-tion, and it simply didn't have any money. It could generate about $3 billion by selling off an investment management division, and as for the rest . . . well, Lehman's management didn't have a lot of solid answers. It was basically $4 billion short.

Earnings calls are strange events—at times they're like kabuki theater, in that they're pretty ritualistic and scripted, and often the one thing that doesn't get discussed is the thing that everyone's wondering about. In this case, the obvious question was where the remaining $4 billion would come from. I was a math geek in college and I know my way around a spreadsheet, but this was the kind of problem that a first grader could spot: *You need seven apples to bake a pie. You only have three apples. How many more apples do you need to pick?*

When the Q&A period of the call came around, I asked a few preliminary questions and then came to the screamingly obvious one: "To the extent you might need $7 billion to capitalize that entity," I said, "and you'll get $3 billion with the spin-off [of the other division], how would you get the other $4 billion?"

The CFO clearly did not want to get nailed down on specifics, so he gave a rambling nonanswer: "Well, we don't feel that we need to raise that extra amount to cover the $7 billion, because you will have less sort of leverageable equity in core Lehman than in, you know, where you are at the end of this quarter."

In other words, Lehman itself had said the plan would cost $7 billion, yet when the numbers didn't add up, suddenly it wouldn't need the whole $7 billion anymore. The real message that came through was that the company was in such dire straits that management had winging it. I'd heard enough, and the next day, September 11, 2008, I downgraded the stock.

Analysts from Citigroup and Goldman downgraded Lehman that same day. Starting with my buy rating from April 2007, Lehman shares had fallen more than 70 percent, to about $4 a share. The sequence of events left me feeling sick to my stomach. This had always been the strike on bad analysts: that we did little more than reflect the current market sentiment, that we would travel in packs, telling you to buy even after the stock price had already soared beyond any reasonable valuation, and telling you to sell only after it had lost most of its value.

The business press occasionally ran stories like this, arguing that we were all a bunch of overpaid losers. I had always tried to separate myself from the crowd, but in this case I had failed, and I had cost my clients money. My two-year track record was still strong—some of the stocks on which I'd placed early sell ratings had declined by 70, 80 or, 90 percent. Still, the mantra on Wall Street is "What have you done for me lately?" I knew this criticism was coming, and I understood that I deserved it. There was nothing to do but take my lumps.

The next day, the *Wall Street Journal* ran a story about the en masse downgrades of Lehman, but I was the only one whose pointillistic portrait ran with the story, looking like a mug shot. I felt that I deserved this—being singled out and made an example of for such an egregious mistake. Shares in Lehman fell 45 percent in one day that week, and it got worse over the weekend, when the federal government decided not to bail out Lehman, and the company went under.

I remember sitting in my office the following morning, stunned. I hadn't thought Lehman would fail, for the same reason I had recommended the stock—I thought its assets held value. However, market forces were at hurricane strength now, and they overwhelmed any kind of systematic evaluation of a company based on its fundamentals.

A member of my team was friendly with a trader within the firm, and when they talked that day, the trader told him that Deutsche Bank was doing very limited business with Morgan Stanley and Goldman Sachs (Goldman Sachs!)—only "on spot" transactions, meaning they had to settle the trade immediately or put up full collateral, in cash. The lack of trust was a common theme for the Street that Monday. That was a sign that the financial system was in serious danger of collapsing.

Lehman's collapse would trigger a devastating and completely unprecedented period on Wall Street. Fannie Mae and Freddie Mac were placed in conservatorship that same month, September 2008. Washington Mutual filed for bankruptcy, and Merrill Lynch was sold to Bank of America. In mid-September, the Securities and Exchange Commission banned shorting of any financial stock. A few weeks later, Wachovia started to run out of liquid funding sources, after enduring a "silent" run on the bank—no hordes of individual depositors demanding their money, just a steady stream of institutions pulling their capital out through electronic channels. Citigroup had an agreement to buy Wachovia—the equivalent of two drunks holding each other up, albeit with a lot of government help—but it ultimately lost the deal to Wells Fargo.

In mid-October, the Treasury Department injected $125 billion in preferred stock in nine large U.S. banks, but even this didn't seem like enough to me. I now pegged the losses for the crisis at around $1 trillion, at a time when the banks had about that much in equity. In other words, if you valued all assets at their current market worth, the industry was likely broke. Because of that, Treasury temporarily suspended the rule that banks had to fairly value their assets. The thinking was that in disorderly markets like this one, the numbers were simply too daunting to calculate.

I was certainly anxious. In addition to sitting on an investment portfolio of 100 percent cash, I took $10,000 out of the bank and hid it in our apartment—an emergency stash in case something really bad happened. I placed this in a file in a dark corner of my home office, under the folder with the tab naming my oldest daughter (yes—my primary thoughts were about providing for my children). Tucked next to each other in that folder were my daughter's Valentine to me from when she was three years old, her acceptance letter to kindergarten, and an envelope with ten grand. I felt a little sheepish about a move like this, but when I mentioned it in passing to a few colleagues, they told me that they'd taken out far more. One client admitted that he'd actually bought gold coins. I also considered selling our condo and renting for a while, a move that my wife vetoed before the words were even out of my mouth.

Meanwhile, New York City was changing. It became steadily easier to find a taxi that fall. Restaurants were noticeably empty. And just as the merger activity among banks had ultimately impacted me a decade earlier, when I was fired after the deal combining Credit Suisse and DLJ, all the fury and confusion swirling around Wall Street would soon show up in my office. Deutsche Bank and other big firms were struggling and needed to lay people off. I'd had a few significant misses— like, obviously, Lehman—yet I still posted my best year ever, because on the whole it was a good time to be negative on bank stocks. The management at Deutsche Bank didn't see it that way, though. Its fixed-income division was suffering, leading to a round of belt-tightening. I thought somewhat bitterly that when the fixed-income guys had a good year they got paid astronomical sums and when they had a bad year we all suffered. Heads they win, and tails we all lose.

■ ■ ■

In hindsight, what's most surprising about the financial crisis is how little of it is actually new. People have done all sorts of investigations and analyses and books about the crisis, and they all identify the same factors: a flood of risky mortgages, banks getting too aggressive about growth, and toothless regulators. Throw in a few other factors, such as interest rates that were too low for too long and overt government support of the housing sector, and you've got most of the root causes.

And yet none of these was some freakish, meteorlike event that flew in from the upper atmosphere. The banking industry has been through boom-and-bust cycles during virtually every period in history over the last 500 years. Certainly, some elements had not been seen for quite a long time, particularly the scope of the problem, large enough to affect not only big banks but small thrifts, investment banks such as Bear Sterns and Lehman, and regular deposit-taking banks. But the elements that made it up were not new. Instead, these were like a new outbreak of an old disease. The fundamental causes of banking crises recur throughout history. It's the same old story of layering risks on top of risks to the point where the entire system becomes unstable.

Risky mortgages? Sure. Unconventional stuff like option adjustable rate mortgages (ARMs), which flipped from low teaser rates to high rates that doubled or tripled monthly payments, were a relatively new product. Bankers from the 1960s and 1970s would have looked at "NINJA" loans, those offered to "no income no job no asset" borrowers, with mouths agape. However, option ARMs weren't really new. Long before the purported "creator" of option ARMs, Angelo Mozillo of Countrywide, was even born, risky home loans were prevalent. In the lead-up to the Great Depression, banks made loans that looked a lot like today's option ARMs. In the 1920s, banks would make home loans to borrowers that were typically five years in length, with effective interest rates as high as 12 to 14 percent, where the borrower would pay just the interest and be expected to pay the balance of the loan in full at the end of the term. In some cases, the loans were "demand" loans, which meant the lender could call the loan—demand full payment of the outstanding balance—at any time. Big fees to refinance these risky loans weren't new, either, with borrowers in the 1920s paying as much as 20 percent of the loan amount to roll over their version of the interest-only mortgage.

That system worked for much of the 1920s, but as soon as home prices started falling—due to unemployment and withering consumer confidence—these homeowners were suddenly unable to refinance.

People faced bills for the entire loan amount at a time when no one was lending. It was the ultimate "credit crunch," and it led to wide swaths of the population losing their houses. When banks took over homes, many eventually collapsed under the weight of bad loans and less valuable real estate. This aspect of the recent crisis is a parallel situation to the Great Depression—in 2011, banks owned as many as 4 million U.S. homes.

In the aftermath of the Great Depression, the thirty-year, fixed-rate mortgage was created. The federal government got involved, creating the Federal Home Loan Banks, a network of institutions that could offer longer-term loans at lower interest rates, with much lower monthly payments. Those thirty-year loans, among other things, succeeded in stabilizing the housing market, and they were ideal for much of the twentieth century. They were predictable for both the borrower and the lender, and their predictability led to the creation of mortgage-backed securities, which allowed institutions to invest in the cash flows created from thirty-year mortgages.

Incidentally, one reason that banks and borrowers started shifting away from thirty-year fixed-rate mortgages was that households started moving more. In an increasingly mobile society, few borrowers end up living in the same house for thirty years, and with interest rates falling and home prices rising, people ended up selling or refinancing their homes more often. As a result, the mortgages got paid off early, and the securities that were based on these mortgages became somewhat less predictable. This can create uncertainty in the instrument, which is something institutional investors don't like.

So for the banking industry, part of the issue was the age-old problem of taking on too much risk. New, untested types of loans were issued, the creditworthiness of borrowers was stretched, and big profits gave the illusion of health. When home prices stopped rising, questionable borrowers were left with ARMs. There was no way those homeowners were going to keep making the payments on their loans.

That wasn't the only thing about the crisis that we had already experienced. The second big factor was banks striving for unhealthy growth rates. This is like a skinny kid wanting to get big fast—you can use steroids to accelerate things beyond the natural growth rate, but only for a while, and usually with pretty serious consequences. Historically, banks have been able to grow revenues about 7 percent a year, close to the growth in nominal gross domestic product, which makes sense. In terms of financial performance, they generated returns of about 1 percent on assets and 10 percent to 12 percent on equity. Slow and steady.

Yet banks usually weren't satisfied with that—they not only wanted to grow, which is healthy, but they wanted to push for overly *aggressive* growth. In that jumbo report I put out in 1999, "Banks and the Red Queen Effect," this was a major theme. After a long expansion in the industry, five years of steady growth thanks to consolidation and eliminating the deadwood, I wanted to know how banks were going to continue that growth. Literally, I just asked them how they planned to do it—most said more loans—and I included a chart of growth projections in the report.

The two most ambitious banks were Citigroup and Fifth Third, both planning to grow earnings 15 percent a year. It's not a coincidence that those two were the worst-performing stocks in the industry over the subsequent decade. It's also not a coincidence that that company with the most conservative growth projections, Wells Fargo, was among the industry's top performers.

Other banks during that period tried to grow by acting like Internet companies. This was during the height of the tech bubble in the late 1990s, when many companies, including banks, looked to position themselves as if they were part tech firm. As a result, banks launched some initiatives that look completely ludicrous in hindsight, like middle-age people trying to learn a trendy new dance. When tech company CMGI's stock was hot (remember that company? the "business incubator" that burned through almost $1 billion?), one bank said that its private equity division should have the same valuation as CMGI. The bank actually used this ridiculous, high-flying, soon-to-flame-out stock as a benchmark.

Another bank announced that it wanted to be a leader in financing the new economy and developing an "Internet company culture." The only problem? This announcement happened in May 2000, roughly two months *after* the all-time peak in the NASDAQ.

In reality, banks should function more like utilities. They should be like the water company—you turn the tap and you know it's going to work. You never hear about a water company executive making

$30 million a year, and the water's never turned off because some trader shorted an aquifer.

I realize that in a public market, banks have to attract investors, and the way you do that is by expanding the company. But all too often, that goal comes at the expense of any kind of risk controls. Banks try to expand not only faster than their competitors but faster than is realistic, sustainable, or safe. When those bets go bad, they can jeopardize the bank's very existence. It's as I learned way back during my earliest training at the Fed: "If something grows like a weed, maybe it is a weed."

Finally, regulators played a huge role in the crisis, in ways that we should have recognized better by now. The oversight of the banking industry has waxed and waned over the past few decades, and just about every time regulators scale back, the banks get into trouble. There are too many examples to name here, but I'll give you one of the most egregious: Darrel Dochow. He worked as a senior bank regulator back in the 1980s, at the predecessor to the Office of Thrift Supervision (OTS). As the S&L crisis was unfolding, Dochow deliberately delayed an investigation into the Lincoln Savings and Loan. Lincoln's CEO, Charles Keating, didn't want the investigation. He threatened legal action if it happened and recruited U.S. Senators to help him out—the notorious Keating Five scandal.

Dochow was just following the orders of his boss, but he was the one who took the action, and it had significant ramifications. Eighteen months later, Lincoln was finally investigated and found to be full of holes: unsafe lending practices, booking inappropriate income, etc. The federal government placed the thrift under conservatorship, in a bailout that cost U.S. taxpayers about $3 billion, and Dochow was demoted because of his role in the incident.

That's not the end of the story. For the next twenty years, Dochow remained at the OTS, where he worked his way back up the institutional ladder. Neither he nor the agency seemed to learn much from the S&L scandal. Among other highlights, Dochow played a key role in helping Countrywide switch regulators in the mid-2000s, from the Office of the Comptroller of the Currency to the OTS. It seems ridiculous that banks get to choose their regulator, but that's often how it works. Agencies compete for banks to gain more power, prestige, and relevance—they try to make themselves appealing by offering a friendlier process and less stringent rules. In the mid-2000s, OTS officials referred to banks as "customers."

By 2007, Dochow had made it all the way back to director of the West Coast division of the OTS—the senior regulator overseeing thrifts that were dead center in the middle of the housing crisis, institutions that generated massive volumes of subprime loans. It was like putting a pyromaniac in charge of the forestry service.

And in 2008, Dochow allegedly helped one of those institutions, IndyMac, backdate some financial records to make it seem stronger than it actually was. The company was running low on cash, putting it at risk of falling to a lower grade with regulators, which would have triggered bigger problems for the company. So, according to a subsequent story in the *Washington Post*, it asked Dochow to sign off on a false document—money that the company wouldn't receive until May would look as if it had been deposited in March. The West Coast director of the OTS, a federal agency, literally helped the company lie.

IndyMac failed not long after that, costing $8.9 billion, according to the Federal Deposit Insurance Corporation, as did Countrywide, Washington Mutual, Downey Savings and Loan, and pretty much every other major thrift on the West Coast—virtually all of the institutions that Dochow and the OTS were supposed to be overseeing. Dochow had to resign in disgrace after the IndyMac debacle became public, this time leaving the agency for good. In the end, not even the agency itself remained; the OTS was absorbed into the Office of the Comptroller of the Currency.

Dochow embodied the buddy-buddy nature of many bank regulators, who view the institutions as clients rather than as entities to be kept in line. His blunders—note the plural—have cost this country billions of dollars, and the most frustrating part of his story is that even something this outrageous was not enough of a scandal to prompt the regulators to change their cozy relationship with the industry.

■ ■ ■

Want more proof? Remember the "global settlement" that Eliot Spitzer and the SEC hashed out back in 2003, which eliminated the worst abuses of stock analysts and banned close ties between them and investment bankers? You'd expect that banks would work to overturn that settlement, under the principle that any regulation is bad, and they have. But you might not expect that the *SEC itself*, the main regulator that helped put the new rules in place, would collaborate with the big banks to undo them.

Yet that's exactly what happened. In the spring of 2010, the SEC joined twelve banks in rewriting the rules to allow closer ties between analysts and investment bankers. This came only seven years after the settlement was struck, and in the wake of the financial crisis, when one of the few things that didn't go wrong was analyst behavior. Luckily, a judge prevented the revision from taking effect. The misguided attempt—regulators working to defang regulation—made it seem as though we've learned nothing from the debacle.

Risky loans, aggressive banks, inept regulators—these are some of the main factors that led to the crisis, yet they're in no way the exception. Far from it, in fact. They're the rule. And they will continue to impact this country. After all, the financial crisis led to dozens of failed banks, hundreds of billions in losses, a global recession, and millions of consumers directly impacted, many of whom lost their homes. If this isn't enough to change the system, what is?

Chapter 7

Citi, Part I:
A Long, Sad Saga

On February 14, 2008, in the midst of the financial crisis, Citigroup CEO Vikram Pandit received a letter from the Office of the Controller of the Currency. This was no Valentine's Day love letter. In eight pages of straightforward language, the OCC regulators who watched over Citi noted several "deficiencies" and "weaknesses" in the way the company managed risk, primarily in the way it had valued and disclosed its holdings in mortgage-backed securities. "It appears management was more focused on short-term performance and profitability along with achieving top industry rankings across many major products rather than on risk or potential loss," the OCC regulators said. "Risk was insufficiently evaluated."

In other words, Citi's internal controls were a mess, and the letter was the government's official notification that the situation was not acceptable. At the time, Pandit had only been in the job a few months.

He had taken over after Chuck Prince stepped down in early November 2007. Typically, when a new CEO takes over for a troubled bank, the market gives the person free rein to come clean about problems and blame the prior management team, and this would have been Pandit's moment to do that. He could have simply said, *OK, this is worse than we thought, but we're going to fix it.*

After all, the company's financial situation was already pretty bad due to risky mortgages. Citi lost $9.8 billion in the fourth quarter of 2007, and the red ink would continue to flow throughout 2008: $5.1 billion, $2.5 billion, $2.8 billion, and $8.3 billion for the four quarters, respectively. Pandit surely knew that Citi still held a boatload of subprime mortgage investments, which were declining in value practically by the day. Coming clean would have bought him some credibility, and it would have alerted investors to a potentially greater risk of future problems. The next time Pandit said something—good news or bad—people would have believed him.

But he didn't. Instead, on February 22, 2008, just eight days after receiving the letter, Pandit signed off on Citi's 10-K, its annual financial report, for the prior year, including a statement saying that the company's internal controls were fine. Pandit knew that, by the standards of a neutral third party, the internal controls were flawed, yet he didn't disclose it. At best he didn't know what was going on and signed off anyway; at worst he committed a lie of omission.

To be clear, regulators en masse deserve as much blame for the financial crisis as anyone else. In a few cases, like at the now-defunct Office of Thrift Supervision, they were way too close to the banks they were supposed to be overseeing, treating them more like clients than objective entities. At the same time, even the good regulators were seriously outnumbered. One estimate calculated that the government had about 80 employees responsible for making sure Citi played by the rules, including the OCC, the Fed, and the SEC. That sounds like an acceptable number of people, but out of over 300,000 total employees, Citi had about 2,000 employees in the risk-management office alone, plus another 2,000 in internal audits, giving the company a 50-to-1 advantage.

In this case, those overwhelmed regulators found something significant. They had done their jobs well, highlighted problems, and communicated those problems to the bank's CEO. Yet their warning was ignored.

Pandit's action in signing the 10-K may have been more than simply dishonest—I believe it was flat-out illegal under the Sarbanes-Oxley Act. As I mentioned, the reason that CEOs now have to personally sign off on financials is because of the 2002 law enacted in response to massive fraud in Enron, WorldCom, and others. Citigroup played a major role in financing and underwriting both Enron and WorldCom and was accused by the SEC of helping Enron hide its debt and artificially boost its profits. Class action suits over those two companies alone cost Citi nearly $5 billion in settlements, a few hundred million more in fines, and untold millions in legal fees. In other words, Citi was a driving force behind the problems that led to the new law.

Sarbanes-Oxley was intended in part to prevent CEOs of companies involved in fraud from pleading ignorance. Instead, they would be personally responsible for reviewing internal controls and attesting to their soundness, and if there was a problem, they would be held responsible. In this instance, at least, it didn't work like that. Pandit's willing disregard for the OCC findings wouldn't become public until early 2011, when the Financial Crisis Inquiry Commission (FCIC) would release some of its reporting into the causes and machinations of the crisis.

Citi denied all implications that Pandit violated Sarbanes-Oxley. The bank's explanation was that the OCC letter never used the key accounting phrase "material weakness," which would have more or less required him to go public with the OCC's findings. But to me, that's splitting hairs. It's a hypertechnical and semantic defense that undercuts the spirit of the law. If Sarbanes-Oxley does not apply here, then it's not clear when it would apply, or what the hundreds of millions of dollars spent on compliance efforts by Citi and other public companies is actually supposed to accomplish.

The entire financial system was in danger, with Citi in the middle, and still holding billions of dollars' worth of the dangerous assets that caused the whole mess. An eight-page letter laying out specific deficiencies and weaknesses in internal controls is significant. That's something you disclose to shareholders. In the opinion of accounting and legal experts I consulted, the letter *did* suffice as notification of "material weakness."

After news of the OCC letter became public in 2011 and I raised alarms, a few tried to play down the issue. *This happened years ago*, they said. *Ancient history.* In my view, though, it's the same CEO, at the head of the same company, which is still foundering years after the financial crisis. His actions then are absolutely relevant to the company's operations today. Moreover, the degree of Pandit's awareness of Citi's weakness in 2008 only became clear in 2011. There is no statute of limitations on treating shareholders poorly.

For the past decade or so, Citi has been involved in virtually every major financial screw-up, from Enron and WorldCom, to the analyst scandals of the tech bubble, to the mortgage fiasco. That long string of setbacks did more than give the company a black eye—it cost Citi shareholders serious money: about $100 billion in pretax losses from fines, settlements, reserves, or write-downs from 2001 to 2010. That works out to about $1 for every $3 made by the company. The lack of consistent management is almost as bad. Even during a period of significant management turnover in the industry, Citi has seen more than its share—since 1998, it has undergone thirty major reorganizations or senior management changes. That includes four CEOs, six CFOs, seven heads of consumer banking, and eight heads of investment banking.

Years ago I wrote in a report to clients that Citi practiced just-in-time risk management, in that it never seemed to spot potential problems until after they blew up, made headlines, and the regulators got involved. That's why the Pandit story is so infuriating. This is a company that has consistently pushed the limits on risky behavior and just as consistently found itself in trouble for it. And yet it doesn't ever seem to fix the root causes, including the corporate culture.

In fact, if you look at the entire history of the company, the past decade doesn't seem like an aberration. The scandals have occurred more frequently—and the dollar amounts are bigger—but they're not new. Citigroup is the Zelig of financial recklessness. It dates back to the early nineteenth century and has come close to failing six times throughout that history, in the years 1921, 1932, 1970, 1982,

1991, and 2008. On multiple occasions, it received federal bailouts to remain solvent, and each of those instances follows a similar arc: The company takes on excessive risks, gets into trouble, and requires the government to step in simply so it can survive. That incident leads to new outside regulations against such risky behavior in the future, which the bank grumbles about and then doesn't follow anyway. Bank industry CEOs who complain of onerous and unnecessary regulation might want to look to Citi first, as it is the poster child for the financial industry's problems, especially over the past three decades.

■ ■ ■

The entity now known as Citigroup was founded almost two centuries ago, in 1812, more than sixty years before Goldman Sachs and more than one hundred years before the Federal Reserve. Back then, it was known as the City Bank of New York, though it would go through several name changes—to Citicorp in 1974 and ultimately to Citigroup in 1998. From the mid-1890s, it has been one of the largest banks, if not *the* largest, in the United States. That dominant position has put it at the center of every major trend in the banking industry, especially during the twentieth century, and many of its strategic decisions are puzzling in hindsight.

In the early 1920s, for example, the company—one of the first in the industry to establish a global footprint—made a huge bet on Cuban sugar producers, along with other U.S. banks. The story illustrates a recurring theme that runs throughout the history of the entire banking sector: the tendency to latch onto one specific asset or strategy that seems to be working and plow resources into it until the enterprise collapses.

Sugar prices soared during and after World War I, and by 1921, the company had lent roughly $79 million to Cuban mills and merchants, representing about 80 percent of its total capital. The Cuban economy boomed thanks to this influx of capital, and then the inevitable happened: Sugar prices plummeted, falling nearly 95 percent in less than a year. The Cuban government established a debt moratorium, which effectively froze any possible principal or interest payments to Citi.

The bank was faced with what would become a familiar problem: If it simply bit the bullet and wrote down the loans—reduced their value on the balance sheet—its capital would be drastically reduced, limiting its ability to extend credit and scaring away customers. The bank would almost certainly go under.

Instead, it kept the loans on its books at full value and actually invested *more* money in the projects, becoming one of the biggest sugar producers in Cuba. Citi securitized some of the debt and sold it to U.S. investors several years later, in the run-up to the crash of 1929. As it turned out, those securities tanked as well, when sugar declined again at the end of that decade. The sugar mills would remain a drag on the company for decades, until they could finally be sold off in 1945. Yet the bank had established a principle that would become part of its operating strategy: When debt goes bad in significant volume, don't default and don't write it down. Instead, just wait it out, throwing good money after bad if needed.

Citi was a major factor in the stock market crash of 1929. By the early 1920s, it exceeded $1 billion in assets—the first U.S. bank to reach this milestone—and the new CEO, Charles Mitchell, would pick up the nickname "Billion Dollar Charlie." The company was heavily involved in both commercial banking and investment banking—that is, it loaned money to companies that it helped bring public while also owning stakes in those companies and pushing its brokers to sell shares in them to the public, through fairly aggressive sales tactics and storefront locations. This arrangement led to all kinds of conflicts of interest, as banks could put a thumb on the scale to give certain companies an unfair advantage, particularly if those companies also happened to be investment banking or commercial lending clients.

Individual investors could buy stocks with as little as 10 percent down, which fueled speculation. Many of those companies soared and then plummeted during the stock market crash of 1929. As Virginia's Senator Carter Glass said of Citi's CEO in November 1929, "Mitchell more than any 50 men is responsible for this stock crash."

The Senate Banking Committee held hearings into the cause of the crash—the so-called Pecora Commission, named after Ferdinand Pecora, chief counsel to the committee. It was that generation's equivalent of the FCIC, and Billion Dollar Charlie was the lead witness, where he was ripped to pieces for his bank's role in the crisis. During his testimony, he admitted that he had made more than $1 million in salary and bonuses in 1929, a year in which he paid no income tax, due to a transaction involving his wife and company stock. It also became clear that the company ran high-pressure sales campaigns to push securities on the public, including some based on the disastrous Cuban sugar properties, where Citi had gone so disastrously wrong earlier in the decade.

Mitchell's testimony could not have come at a worse time—it took place during the banking crisis of 1933, during which 38 states had shut down their banks and the remaining 10 states had put in place strict limits that let people withdraw only 5 to 10 percent of their money. The contrast between this swaggering bank CEO, earning in excess of $1 million a year, and the day-to-day experience of most Americans was stark, and five days after the hearings, he stepped down as CEO. Still, while the Depression forced hundreds of smaller institutions out of business, Mitchell's bank survived, in large part because of government policies designed to prop up the financial sector.

The Pecora Commission led to wide-ranging reforms on Wall Street, including the Glass-Steagall Act, which became law in 1934 and separated commercial banking from investment banking. The act was cosponsored by Carter Glass, the senator who had directly blamed Mitchell for the crisis. Citi sold off its securities operation and focused on deposits. Other New Deal reforms included the establishment of the Federal Deposit Insurance Corporation (FDIC), which was intended to prevent bank runs, and a law called Regulation Q, which limited the interest that banks could pay on short-term deposits, such as savings and checking accounts. The thinking was that banks would have competed by offering ever-increasing interest rates, and consumers would chase the highest rate, destabilizing the financial system.

These reforms would lead to a period of relative stability in finance that lasted more than four decades. While the U.S. economy expanded, banks were there to finance that growth, without major credit crunches, panics, or financial meltdowns. Banks were slow and steady and reliable. They weren't fantastic investments, but they provided liquidity and credit for the economy, and they were stable.

■ ■ ■

The next notable CEO at the company was Walter Wriston, who joined in 1946 as a loan officer and was CEO from 1967 until 1984. Wriston hated the New Deal philosophy and the strictures it placed on the banking industry, which he felt were overly burdensome. As he rose through the company, he developed new products that helped circumvent the rules. Looking at Regulation Q, which restricted the interest paid on short-term deposits, he saw that the bank would not grow sufficiently until it could attract deposits in greater volume. So he came up with something called a negotiable certificate of deposit (CD).

Businesses and foreign customers, who weren't subject to the same rules as U.S. accounts, could put $100,000 into something that looked a lot like a basic savings or checking account—the money earned interest, and depositors could pull it out at any time by simply selling the CD into a secondary market. At the time, there was no secondary market, but Wriston solved that problem. He found a bond dealer in New York who said he would need a loan of $10 million to make a market in the new CDs. Wriston had Citi sign off on the loan and established the market, and then Citi started selling negotiable CDs.

Wriston pretty much created the whole market from scratch, and he deliberately did not ask for clearance from the Fed, under the theory that it's easier to ask for forgiveness than to ask for permission. It worked. By this point, three decades after the Great Depression, the Fed wanted to make sure the banks had enough money to operate and that depositors, especially commercial depositors, would not have to pull their money and put it into some other product or account to get a higher interest rate. The new product would guarantee this. Citi started offering the CDs in 1961, quickly followed by most other major banks, and in the first year they drew about $1 billion in deposits for the industry. The new CD funds would aid a spate of new loans, with overall lending increasing by half from 1962 to 1965, reaching $200 billion.

That's a notable achievement, but there's a catch—that kind of loan growth was much faster than the country's overall economic growth in the same time period, a split that's inherently unsustainable. Banks were putting their foot on the accelerator, and for reasons that often seem to make sense for bankers: When you make a lot of loans, you make a lot of money. Credit is the product that banks sell, and when they're selling that product in high volume, they're happy. At least, they're happy when those loans go out the door. The trick lies in is getting all those borrowers to pay the money back.

As you can probably guess, that didn't always happen. In 1970, the bank had huge exposure to Penn Central, the railroad company. The debt was in the form of commercial paper, the short-term loans (typically thirty days or less, sometimes overnight) that businesses use to cover immediate operating expenses. Investors buy these loans as a reasonably safe place to park their money, and banks make fees by facilitating the deals. From 1968 to 1970, the amount of commercial paper in the United States more than doubled, to almost $40 billion. But in June of that year, Penn Central hit a major cash crunch and defaulted on about $80 million in commercial paper.

The problem was severe enough that the entire commercial paper market seized up. Investors no longer wanted to buy it, not from Penn Central or from any corporation. Wriston, the same executive who railed against the New Deal as an unnecessary intrusion into the market, now called the Fed and begged for help. He argued that with commercial paper temporarily frozen, banks would need to borrow through other means, and he convinced the Fed to keep the discount window, which allows banks to borrow money, available over the weekend, an extremely rare occurrence. The Fed agreed—bailing out Citi and the rest of the commercial banking industry—and managed to prevent the crisis from spreading. This would be the first of several instances in Wriston's career when he stopped demanding that the government get off his back and started demanding that it come to his aid.

■ ■ ■

Among his other dreams, Wriston wanted to turn his company into a growth stock, like other high-fliers at the time, such as IBM.

In 1971, he set a public goal of increasing earnings by 15 percent annually, and he actually delivered on it for the next few years, in part by increasing lending to new heights and setting aside smaller reserves in case those loans went bad. As former *New York Times* financial columnist Jeff Madrick put it in his book *The Age of Greed*, Wriston argued that "the banks did not need minimum capital requirements set by government because his bankers knew a lot more about the riskiness of their loans than government examiners did."

Yet that wasn't always true. In the mid- to late 1970s, the company loaned in significant volume to companies that quickly ran into trouble, such as tanker companies (which suffered during the oil crisis), real estate (impacted by the recession), and even citizens-band radio manufacturers (the 1970s version of dot-com stocks). In 1977, Citi suffered its first loss since the Great Depression. Yet it would continue to lend aggressively.

In the late 1970s and early 1980s, developing markets became the next area to finance. These were countries, primarily in Latin America, that were considered risky but could generate higher interest rates. They were the original subprime borrowers—if you can't lend to the "prime" countries, try Brazil and Mexico. Wriston had an infrastructure advantage in this market, in the form of a global network of loan officers. And he lobbied the Treasury Department to ease the rules regarding loans to foreign markets. Treasury complied, and debt to these countries started flowing. Since then, this expansion outside the United States has proved either lucrative or problematic, depending on the phase of the business cycle.

In classic form, U.S. banks recognized an opportunity, one aspect of the banking world that seemed to be working, and poured money into it until it stopped working. That's capitalism—exploit favorable market returns until they're diminished—but Citi kept pushing even after they turned negative. At one point, Citibank had sovereign loans to Brazil alone that amounted to 83 percent of its total capital. This echoed the Cuban sugar debacle from decades earlier, when it put about 80 percent of its capital into loans to Cuban sugar producers. In August 1982, Mexican officials went to Washington to announce that the country could no longer make its interest payments. Other countries followed—the entire sector of "lesser developed countries" ran into trouble all at once, and U.S. banks suddenly had a clutch of bad loans on their books.

It was the biggest financial crisis since the 1920s. And again, Wriston—who largely wanted to be left alone by government, feeling that regulations on the industry were overly burdensome—came running for help when the market turned against him. If these loans were pegged at their actual value, two major banks (Manufacturer's Hanover and Chemical, both of which are part of JPMorgan today) would have been wiped out and several others would have been severely crippled. Instead, the U.S. government put together a package of more loans, and it deferred the repayment of some others. The International Monetary Fund got involved. Commercial banks would be required to put in $5 billion, merely so that Mexico and other borrower countries could make the interest payments on their old debt. It was like giving a strapped consumer with a wallet full of maxed-out credit cards a new one just to cover the minimum payments on the others.

In the midst of this crisis in 1982, Wriston attempted to calm investors and regulators by writing an op-ed piece in the *New York Times* arguing that a "country does not go bankrupt." It would become his most notorious phrase, and in a weird and somewhat irrelevant way, he was right. As he explained it, countries own more than they owe. If they sold all of their assets, they would have enough to pay off all of their debts, making bankruptcy an impossibility. That was a technical point based on wording however. The bottom line was that the borrowers couldn't pay the money back. The loans were bad. End of story.

The U.S. government, in addition to structuring the bailout packages, gave the banks explicit permission to continue valuing their Latin American debt at full face value. With official clearance to ignore the problem, banks were allowed to maintain far lower reserves against probable losses on these loans than they should have. The government basically eased accounting standards and capital requirements, specifically to help the banks weather the crisis. As a result, Citibank was able to pretend it had a pretty good year in 1982, with earnings up 35 percent, a significant fiction given that about a third of its assets were now in cross-border loans. In some cases the maneuvers required for the countries to appear current on their debt and for the banks to document their up-to-date status became ludicrous. Argentina received a bailout similar to Mexico's bailout—new loans to pay off the interest on its old loans—and the money went into and out of the country on the same day, December 2, 1983.

Wriston ultimately retired as CEO in September 1984, after seventeen years at the top of Citi. He was a giant in the world of banking, a forward thinker and pioneer who laid a foundation for global growth that continues today. Yet his legacy was tainted by the Latin American debt crisis, which would continue to haunt Citi's books for years. The new CEO, John Reed, finally took a $3 billion write-down against the company's Latin American debt in 1987. By that point, the company had recovered to a point that it was able to withstand such a move. The company's shares actually rose on the news, probably out of sheer relief on the part of investors. The U.S. government would put more money into the problem—loaning an additional $20 billion to borrower countries, allowing them to service their debt and giving U.S. banks a cushion. The industry didn't solve the problem; it merely stalled for a few years until that problem was no longer as relevant.

Wriston truly transformed banking—for better and for worse. He never wanted to work at a traditional bank, and he got his wish, creating a new kind of financial company that could dream up innovative solutions, such as the automatic teller machine, for which he deserves tremendous credit. Yet he also pushed the limits of the sector, creating a massive company with undue influence in Washington. He was the ultimate insider, pulling strings with connections at the Treasury Department (twice he was offered the top job in that agency), in order to ensure that his bank did not suffer the full consequences of some of its most foolish decisions. In this way, Wriston was a model for the modern banking system.

■ ■ ■

Despite Wriston's achievements, Sandy Weill is the person most directly responsible for Citi in its current structure. Weill didn't have Wriston's ability to foster new products, but he did have the ability to make deals and cut costs and nearly matched Wriston's degree of influence in Washington. Beginning his career as a runner on the stock trading floor, he cofounded a tiny brokerage company and turned it into one of the largest securities firms on Wall Street—Shearson Loeb Rhoades—which he later sold to American Express. Between 1986 and 2003, he completed more than a hundred acquisitions to create Citigroup, a kind of financial supermarket where both retail consumers and companies could handle all of their needs—banking, credit cards, mortgages, insurance, investment banking, commercial lending, you name it. The defining moment was the late 1998 marriage between Travelers Group, with Weill at the helm, and Citicorp, then led by CEO John Reed.

To get the merger done, Weill and Reed lobbied hard to overturn the Glass-Steagall Act. They had some help from others in the banking industry, the media, and even some within government, such as Robert Rubin, President Clinton's Treasury Secretary. It was more than a little ironic that Citi, the company perhaps most responsible for the passage of Glass-Steagall, would argue to repeal it. Imagine if Barry Bonds's grandson were to argue someday that the rules regarding drug testing in sports needed to be scaled back a bit, and you get the idea.

The Citi/Travelers merger was announced in 1998; at that point, it was the largest corporate merger in history. The deal was signed not only before the ink was dry on the repeal of Glass-Steagall but before the ink had even been put on paper. The new organization's massive corporate structure proved extremely difficult to integrate, though, given that it was combining different corporate cultures, technologies, and financial processes. This was no doubt complicated by the fact that the Travelers entity that Weill brought was a roll-up itself, a bunch of formerly independent companies bolted together.

It didn't help that the new company had two CEOs, Weill and Reed, and three presidents. I started calling the company Noah's Ark in research reports, given that Citi seemed to have two managers for every department. Weill set extremely ambitious growth targets that required doubling profits every five years. That kind of growth is possible only in the short term, by making many more loans and cutting corners in risk management. Weill did it primarily through acquisitions, more than by improving the operating performance of the entities the company already owned.

I didn't think the new merger was off to a strong start, and I suggested as much in my reports to clients. In response, the company began reducing my access to management, a systematic freeze-out that wouldn't end until 2003.

From late 2001 through the end of 2002, I was conspicuously ignored on all Citigroup conference calls. I also failed to secure any meetings with management, even as analysts who were more positive got more than one. One of my competitors during this period would later write Weill's 2006 authorized biography. Citigroup repeated a line that I had heard a few years earlier when I asked to meet with management: Why would this be a good use of our time?

In other words, I was shut out. In private meetings with investors, I had described Citigroup as having "economies of clout"—as opposed to economies of scale—given its ability to wield its trillion dollars of assets to influence the media, regulators, analysts, and others, and I was feeling the blunt end of this force.

Finally, in October 2002, I put a disclaimer in my reports to draw attention to the way the company was treating me. I intended it to read like a black box warning placed by the Food and Drug Administration on the package of a risky new drug. It read: *The reader should be aware that the analyst has had very little direct contact with management since the beginning of the year, either in the form of one-on-one meetings with members of Citigroup's management team or participation in the Q&A sessions on investor conference calls sponsored by Citigroup.*

This finally got the company's attention. A few investors from big mutual fund companies called Citigroup to complain. After releasing several reports with this disclaimer over a few weeks, I finally got a call from Citigroup, during which I was asked, "What will it take to make you get rid of this line?" I got my meeting, which helped me better understand the corporate strategy, but I didn't change my negative conclusion about the company's prospects. At one point, I had suggested that the company was dipping into the cookie jar to hit its earnings targets—that is, it was pulling money from unconventional sources to make up for poor operating performance. When I finally had a meeting with the CFO, to break the ice I brought him a bag of cookies.

■ ■ ■

It was little solace that the people who were likely responsible for excluding me didn't stick around long at Citi. One president and the head of investor relations resigned in the mid-2000s. The CFO who ate the cookie at the meeting would later be forced out during a management shuffle and an alleged disagreement with then–CEO Chuck Prince. Of course, Prince wouldn't last, either.

It was also cold comfort that I was increasingly proven right about Citigroup, as the company began experiencing a range of problems, both small and large. Citigroup spun off a significant part of its Travelers insurance division in 2002 because it felt that this business was hurting its stock price. The company continued to have issues integrating different systems and divisions. As part of my kick-the-tires research, I walked into a Citi branch in Manhattan in 2003 and asked if I could apply for a credit card. The branch employee handed me a pamphlet and told me to call the 800 number. That meant the banking and credit card systems were not linked and the sales effort was not coordinated. So much for the financial supermarket.

The analyst scandals related to technology stock recommendations erupted around this period. Citi was the prime offender, paid the largest settlement, $400 million, and was forced to fire several analysts. The Enron and WorldCom implosions came around the same time, underscoring the problems inherent in connecting commercial and investment banking. In Enron's dying days, when it was having a hard time securing short-term credit to fund its daily operations, Citi reportedly offered to lend the company a big chunk of money in exchange for the right to handle all of its underwriting business in the future. This showed the degree to which some investment bankers would do a deal with anybody, even zombie companies, if they thought it would generate a fee.

In the midst of these problems, I made another prediction: Wall Street would face $10 billion in legal costs. At the time, that was an unheard-of amount, higher than the legal costs for any other banking scandal in history. Among my peers, the next closest prediction was in the hundreds of millions—an order of magnitude lower—and I found out later that some skeptics were referring to me as a shock analyst. I knew the $10 billion number wasn't perfect, but I thought that a potentially inaccurate estimate was better than none, since investors need to consider extreme but probable outcomes, or risk losing a lot of money.

The estimate came up at one conference that Citigroup sponsored for its major investing clients. It was held at the Plaza Hotel in

New York, with an overflow crowd, and CEO Sandy Weill delivered the keynote address. My team and I listened through an Internet broadcast, as required by Regulation FD, which required companies to offer webcasts of these events to anyone who wanted to listen. No more secret handshakes among the insiders. Weill's speech talked about Citigroup's strategy and finances, and during the Q&A session afterward, an investor asked what he thought about "Mike Mayo's prediction of legal costs of $10 billion."

In my office, I looked at my colleagues in amazement. After a brief delay, Weill said, "Two years ago, Mike Mayo came looking for a job and didn't get it. I've been paying for it ever since." The audience got the joke and laughed; I considered this response a compliment. It's more important to be respected than to be liked on Wall Street, and at a minimum, the estimate was respected. In fact, despite continued criticism of that $10 billion number, it ended up being correct two years later, when many companies on Wall Street took big charges to their earnings due to the scandals. Citi alone paid more than $5 billion.

There were other, less publicized—though no less unsavory—screw-ups to follow. In 2004, regulators in Japan accused employees in Citi's private bank division of less-than-ethical sales practices and making loans to some clients that were used to manipulate stocks. The company had been warned about practices like this in Japan dating all the way back to 2001. Private banking in Japan was a tiny division that didn't even earn much revenue, but the story made headlines worldwide. CEO Chuck Prince had to personally fly to Japan to apologize to bank regulators there, though they pulled Citi's license anyway.

That same year, 2004, Citi spread some love to Europe, where traders set out to destabilize the corporate bond market by selling billions in bonds in less than two minutes, causing prices to fall so that they could immediately buy up a big chunk of those bonds at a lower price a half hour later, netting about $18 million in profits. The strategy was called "Dr. Evil," after the villain in the Austin Powers movies, but this was no comedy: It resulted in another round of negative headlines and a fine of more than $10 million, which, granted, is a drop in the bucket in terms of Citi's regulatory expenses over the years. As the *Independent* newspaper put it, British regulators who looked into the trade said that Citi's "internal controls were remiss," which by now had become a familiar problem.

■ ■ ■

Of course, the recent financial crisis was an encapsulated version of all of these issues—Citi's long, sad history applied to the twenty-first century. Let's go down the checklist.

Financial shenanigans? Check. In the mid-2000s, Citi got more deeply into toxic mortgage investments than almost any other bank on Wall Street, and near the peak of the market, meaning it didn't get to reap as much of the hefty fees that drew most big banks to mortgage-backed securities in the first place.

Less than transparent disclosure? Yep. When securities backed by subprime mortgage assets started to turn bad, the company understated its exposure by about $40 billion in a conference call with investors. The details of that last incident are complicated, but the short version is that when Citi was securitizing and selling CDOs, it offered buyers something called a liquidity put, which was akin to a money-back guarantee. If the market for such securities started to have problems, the puts established that Citi would buy them back at a prearranged price. It was a sweetener, and it worked—the securities were more attractive to buyers but also more dangerous for Citi.

By mid-2007, investors were increasingly demanding information about the bank's exposure to these securities. During the company's second-quarter earnings call, management said that its subprime exposure actually declined by 45 percent since the end of 2006, to $13 billion. It neglected to mention that there was another $40 billion out there, due to the liquidity puts, super-senior tranches, and other factors, that could potentially come home to roost.

That oversight led to yet another lawsuit, this one from the SEC, which resulted in a settlement of $75 million. The lawsuit strongly hinted that Rubin and Prince, along with several other Citi executives, knew of the growing losses on even the highest-rating mortgage-backed assets, although it didn't accuse any of those executives of anything illicit. Citi's defense was that it was under "no obligation to say anything about its 'subprime exposure'" during that frenzied period in 2007, though it voluntarily decided to offer some information to shareholders, to give them a "more concrete understanding." The CFO who spoke on that call paid $100,000 in fines and the head of investor relations paid $80,000; neither admitted any wrongdoing, and neither is at Citi any longer.

Next up on the historical parallel checklist? A bailout. Citi got a jumbo bailout, the mother of all bailouts, the biggest in the industry. In fact, that should be plural—it got *bailouts*, multiple instances of direct and extraordinary intervention from the federal government, expressly because the country's most senior regulators were convinced in November 2008 that Citi was on the brink of going under, and they were probably right. CDS spreads on the company's debt—a measure of the chance that a company will fail—were widening rapidly, doubling to 5 percent in one week alone. More ominous, customers around the world were pulling their cash at accelerating rates that gave the company just a few weeks to survive. To shore up the company's finances, the U.S. government injected its second wave of Troubled Asset Relief Program (TARP) funds, $20 billion, at year-end 2008, only a few months after an initial round of bailout funds, when Citi got $25 billion.

The regulators—Fed chairman Ben Bernanke, New York Fed president Tim Geithner, Treasury Secretary Hank Paulson, Comptroller of the Currency John Dugan, and head of the FDIC, Sheila Bair—decided that Citi had to be saved no matter what, and they crafted a package of nearly $350 billion in assistance. That included preferred equity investments of $45 billion (the TARP funds) and $301 billion in asset guarantees. Citi also benefited from government programs that guaranteed commercial paper at times. Citi ultimately paid back the government, but there were other lasting costs due to the bailouts Citi and others received, such as the need for lower interest rates that cost savers returns on their deposits, and will likely continue to do so through 2014.

This would be the biggest bailout in Citi's long history, and while the government's actions succeeded in ensuring the company's survival, it was done in a manner—in the words of subsequent government reports that looked into the treatment of Citi—that was "strikingly ad hoc." The regulators made a decision that Citi was too systemically important to be allowed to fail, yet there were no objective criteria for that decision. It was a hunch, based on the size and scope of Citi and the market's reaction to the failure of Lehman Brothers.

Moreover, the government's actions created a clear moral hazard, in that nobody was truly punished for pushing Citi to the brink. No C-suite executive, no risk officer, no trader or broker—no one. And the unavoidable conclusion that the federal government serves as a de facto backstop for companies like Citi gives them an inherent advantage, in that it helps them borrow money at lower rates. Citi's shareholders didn't lose everything in the financial crisis, but they came close. Yet bondholders suffered no similar fate. The terms of the bailout guaranteed that they would remain whole, getting 100 cents on the dollar for all of Citi's debt. From now on, that lack of market risk—the implicit guarantee of the U.S. federal government—is at least partly priced into the company's cost of capital, making it lower than it otherwise would be.

Finally, as during many events in the company's history, soft regulation played a role this time, as well. Citi was able to put itself in so much danger during the crisis because it ignored not only its own historical precedents but also specific warnings from regulators. The letter that Pandit received in February 2008 wasn't the first warning from the OCC. More than two years earlier, in December 2005, Citi had received another letter from the same agency, warning of outsize risks in the bond division—the same one that would later securitize those mortgage-backed assets. Additional critical letters would come. In May 2008, the Federal Reserve Bank of New York—a separate agency from the OCC—wrote Citi a memo requiring that it create a risk management plan. The fact that the company received these letters didn't come out until the wake of the crisis; they were released as part of the FCIC's final report.

In other words, the news of problems within the company's risk management office wasn't really news at all. It was part of a longer series of back-and-forth maneuvers in which government regulators tried to keep up with the company, and Citi made just enough changes to keep them at bay while ignoring the root of the problem. Why didn't the regulators do more? They were simply overwhelmed. As one

put it, "Citigroup was earning \$4 to \$5 billion a quarter, and that is
really hard for a supervisor to successfully challenge."

■ ■ ■

Here's how I know that nothing's really changed at Citi: Even after
multiple bailouts, multiple incidents in which it was saved from almost
certain bankruptcy only by forceful government intervention, the company still has strong disdain for criticism, even if it's grounded in fact.
There's little humility, little caution, little recognition that Citi has
burned through its goodwill and might have to work a little harder to
convince regulators and investors and the public at large that it learned
from its many mistakes and will make sure that it doesn't repeat them.

This is something I would experience firsthand, during a long
standoff with Citi during most of 2010, when it became clear to me
that the company wasn't merely dragging its heels on reform—it was
actively refusing to listen to criticism.

Chapter 8

Citi, Part II:
The Plot Sickens

Something that Vikram Pandit said in mid-2010 set a new bar for absurdity. It happened during a conference call in July, when Citi was discussing its earnings for the second quarter of the year and its goals for the future. The company had recently announced growth targets, which seemed overly ambitious to me. These aren't just numbers that the company pulls out of a hat—they come from a long process in which mid-level managers look at their operations and decide what kind of growth rate is realistic. The numbers get combined and refined by senior managers and ultimately the board, and finally the CEO and CFO sign off on them.

Citigroup had announced its goals during a presentation a few months earlier, back in March. Specifically, the goals were listed on slide 29 of the presentation. (I don't forget things like this.) One of Citigroup's goals—there were only two—was to increase assets

131

on its Citicorp business by 5 percent. That doesn't sound high, but if you look back at the history of banks, it's pretty reckless to give any target based on the growth of assets. For a bank, a loan is an asset, which can be confusing to those outside the banking world. Banks grow assets by making more loans—essentially asking "Who wants money?" They can hit or even exceed growth targets for a while by lending aggressively, which is not hard to do. That was one of the major driving factors that led to Citi's problems during the financial crisis: trying to grow assets at the expense of things like safety and soundness. Over the past decade, no other big bank had set such aggressive goals—15 percent earnings growth, under former CEO Sandy Weill—or had gotten into such trouble because of them.

At the same time, the company suffers from the law of large numbers. For a company with assets of $1.4 trillion in the targeted growth area, a 5 percent increase means generating upward of $70 billion in new business every year, equivalent to half a percent of total U.S. gross domestic product. Citigroup was aiming for that kind of growth during a slumping global economy. Much of a bank's growth—any bank's—depends on the overall economy, which even the most talented executive can't control. Citi's 5 percent goal was like a hitter in baseball saying he's going to go three for four in a particular game before he even knows who's pitching.

So the new target was probably worth a question on the earnings call, right?

I thought so. When my turn came around (sixth, which actually wasn't as low in the order as I had expected), I asked Pandit about that number. "Why have any financial target at all that's focused on asset growth?" I said. "Especially when Citigroup, one could say, grew assets too aggressively last decade?"

Pandit's response was a triumph of Lewis Carroll logic: "It's not a target," he said. "It's an outcome of what we think is going to happen because of the markets that we're in." In other words, the company not only issued what many people would say is a misguided projection, but its executives weren't even standing up for it. Instead, Pandit's approach was to say, *That's not a goal. It's not something we're reaching for—we're so well positioned that we're merely going to be the passive recipient of that growth.* Nice. Like manna from heaven.

■ ■ ■

That exchange on the conference call was only one part of a year-long standoff between Citigroup and me. Starting in October 2009, I repeatedly aired out a number of dubious things the company was doing and was repeatedly ignored or punished for daring to raise these topics. Citi's stubborn reaction was baffling to me: If any company would want to keep its nose clean around that time, you'd think it would be this one, after its long streak of financial misadventures.

I knew that Citi was taking some risky steps with basic accounting standards. The gist was that Citigroup had so-called deferred tax assets on its books. These are akin to credits from the IRS. If a company loses money in a given year, it gets to use those losses to reduce its tax bill on profits in the future.

It's almost like a mulligan in golf—the IRS says, "OK, you had a bad year, but if things turn around for you, we'll give you a break next year." (There's a similar concept in place for retail investors, by the way. If you buy stock in a company and lose money, you can use that loss to offset capital gains in the future.) Until you use those credits, they sit on your balance sheet, and just as the name suggests, you can count them as assets.

Citigroup's situation in mid-2009 was a little different. The company had been in such bad shape that it was sitting on roughly $40 billion worth of tax credits, or more than a third of its core equity. Citi had lost so much money in the three years after the collapse of the U.S. housing market that those credits were among the most valuable things it owned. That's right: One of the best things about Citi at the time was the fact that it had done so badly.

These tax credits don't last forever. They have a shelf life, and if a company posts three years of losses in a row, as was the case at Citi, it typically has to reduce the credits' value on the balance sheet. The company officially states that the credits are not actually worth $40 billion anymore, they're worth something less. One accounting expert told me that nine out of ten companies in a similar situation will take such a step. General Motors was the only other corporation with such a large magnitude of deferred tax assets, $53 billion, partly because it suffered through a few brutal years during the recession. Like Citigroup, it had survived only because of the intervention of the federal government, which took a large ownership stake. Like Citigroup, it would return to profitability in 2010, just barely, though it wasn't likely to make the big profits of its past anytime soon.

Result? GM bit the bullet and wrote down the value of its tax credits, from $53 billion all the way down to $8 billion. That's $45 billion in assets. Let's be clear, though—these are paper losses, as when your house is appraised at value X and a few years later it's worth value Y. No one took money out of your pocket, but your assets are worth less. I'm not going to argue that this is a pleasant experience, but there's also no point pretending that the number is higher than it really is. As of late 2011, Citi's deferred tax assets remain the largest discretionary accounting entry in the company's history. Indeed, in September 2011, Harvard Business School would consider Citi's tax issue important enough that it devoted a case study on the topic.

The company's deferred tax asset situation was just another example of how Citi was still pushing the envelope in terms of its risk management. As a result, I put out a research report saying the company might have to take a write-down of as much as $10 billion, or around one-fourth of the value. I've published thousands of reports over the decades. Sometimes the market simply shrugs, but not this time.

The report got covered on CNBC that afternoon. Even at a company the size of Citigroup, with $2 trillion in assets, $10 billion is the kind of number that gets people's attention, and the stock started dropping immediately. By the end of the day, shares would close down more than 5 percent.

That didn't win me any more fans at Citigroup. As mentioned, the company had refused to let me meet with management early in the prior decade and, while I had been negative on Citi at a time when the stock was rising, the financial crisis had validated some of my worst suspicions about it and other banks on Wall Street. But somehow that didn't earn me any credibility with the people inside Citi. Instead, it only made them dig their heels in. For the rest of 2009 and most of 2010, Citigroup effectively refused to meet with me despite having meetings with multiple other analysts, some several times.

And as of mid-2010, when it was busy issuing growth nontargets like the one Pandit denied, Citigroup was still more than 25 percent owned by the federal government. Meaning it wasn't just Citi shareholders who were potentially being harmed by the company's mismanagement but ordinary American taxpayers.

The parallels between 2002 and 2010 were almost eerie. During the earlier standoff, when I testified before the Senate Banking Committee at hearings related to the Sarbanes-Oxley Act, I thought that having a high-profile opportunity to speak my mind meant that a company like Citigroup couldn't just pretend I didn't exist.

In January 2010, when I testified at the first day of hearings of the Financial Crisis Inquiry Commission, I was the first to speak after lead-off testimony by CEOs from Goldman Sachs, Merrill Lynch, JPMorgan, and Bank of America as a check on the statements they made. Much of the financial creativity of the past decade, I said, was like bad sangria: "A lot of cheap ingredients repackaged to sell at a premium. It might taste good for a while, but you get headaches later and you have no idea what's really inside." For a brief moment, I felt that my views were taken seriously and that Citi could not again simply ignore me. I was wrong again.

■ ■ ■

In April 2010, a client of mine who works in the hedge fund industry confirmed that Citi was deliberately excluding me. Over the phone, he talked about a visit he'd made to the company recently and then added, "It seems like you're frozen out over there." I was stunned—they'd apparently said something to him about my situation. When I asked Citi about this, they maintained the party line that I was being treated like all other analysts.

In June, I actually approached Pandit and a team of his senior managers in the lobby of a large investment firm in Boston. I happened to be visiting some money managers that day when I heard that Pandit would be in the building for an event that started at noon. After my meetings were over, I camped out at a Starbucks in the lobby with a banana and a yogurt until he arrived.

Suddenly I saw Pandit and his team walk in. I walked diagonally across the lobby, shoes clicking, and intercepted them by the turnstiles. "Vikram," I said, extending a hand. "Mike Mayo."

He smiled, shook my hand, and asked what he could do for me. I should point out here that, at least on my end, none of this is personal. Pandit seems to be a genuinely decent person—thoughtful and upbeat. In person, he seems more like a research scientist than the CEO of one of the biggest banks in the world.

"I'd like to come in and meet with management," I said. "It's been almost two years."

Pandit looked around at the senior executives surrounding him. "Anyone have a problem with that?" he asked. Silence. "Then it's settled. You'll have a meeting."

I couldn't let it go at that. "I've been hearing that for a year," I said. "In all that time, I haven't been given a firm date, and it would be helpful to put something down."

Pandit just offered an enigmatic smile and moved with his group toward the elevators. Maybe I was being naive, but I honestly thought that this was binding, since he had given me his word in person. When I triumphantly returned home with this news and told my wife, she said that he was swatting away a gnat, and that I was the gnat in question. I disagreed. I had his word on it, in person, eye to eye, in an exchange that would be considered binding in almost any time and place.

My wife was right. For another two months, nothing. In July, on the earnings conference call, Citi responded to my first question about the firm's prospects. I then also asked about the status of my meeting, in front of the hundreds of investors on the call. Silence. By the end of the summer, I'd had enough. I had spoken with several tax experts who felt that the rules on deferred tax assets were clear—and that Citi wasn't following them. I found that the SEC had also looked into the issue, as had the inspector general of TARP. The former chief accountant of the SEC, Lynn Turner, was quoted in the *Financial Times* about the tax assets, saying that "Citi's position defies imagination and logic."

Soon the media picked up the story, including Fox Business News and CNBC. A few print outlets, such as the *Wall Street Journal*, ran articles as well. The *New York Post* announced, "The gloves are off in analyst's feud with Citi," and the story beneath called me "a gruff researcher" who prides himself in not pandering to companies. One *Wall Street Journal* blogger said, "Mr. Mayo is right to be skeptical. He has been covering Citi longer than anyone running it."

Finally Citigroup relented, saying in the press that I would have my meeting "after Labor Day." Initially the company refused to provide a date, leading Charlie Gasparino, the business journalist and Fox Business News commentator, to joke that "Citi said they'd meet with Mike Mayo after Labor Day. They just didn't say what year."

It wasn't until October 1 that I finally had my meeting. I was surprised that advance coverage in the *New York Times*' included a mention about my choice of tie.

■ ■ ■

That Friday morning, I was up at 4:30 A.M. with energy to burn on pull-ups at the gym. At slightly before 1 P.M. that afternoon, I met with the nine investors I'd been allowed to bring with me. We gathered in the lobby at 399 Park Avenue, Citi's headquarters, and rode the elevator to the second-floor conference room. The CFO went around the long conference table and shook hands with everyone, followed by the CEO, Pandit. This was the first time I'd ever met this CFO in person—the sixth that Citi has had in the past decade—and he avoided eye contact, moving on quickly.

I began by simply saying "I'm here to learn." I pointed out that I had some concerns, most of which they probably knew about—in addition to the press coverage, I'd sent over a list of questions in advance—but I explained that before we got into those things, I wanted to hear what was going well. Pandit spoke for a few moments about the ongoing reorganizing of the company, the sale of poorly performing units, growth in developing markets, and so on.

When it was my turn to talk, I asked Pandit again about the company's 5 percent growth target in assets, showing the slide from the company's presentation back in March that specifically labeled this as a goal. He didn't answer. Instead another Citi manager in the room asked me, "Did you read the transcript?" I said that I did, and he then recited lines from the transcript of that earnings call aloud, stating that it was not a goal but rather a natural consequence of the markets they were in.

The manager next explained that the company's real goal was the other target on the same slide: not growth in assets but return on assets (ROA) of 1.25 percent to 1.5 percent. This is also quite high—historically, banks return about 1 percent on assets, and Citi's number lately had been closer to 0.9 percent. But the company was trying to sell off its worst-performing pieces and applying that ROA number just to the good stuff left behind. As I had written in a research note, that's like throwing out the five worst holes of a round of golf and basing a prediction of your future scores on the remaining 13. The world doesn't work that way, and even if it did, Citi was asking investors to believe that all of its mistakes were behind it.

The rest of the meeting went much of the same way. I would ask a question of Pandit and another executive would answer, conceding nothing. Parts of the conversation were civil, and at one point we even laughed a little. But mostly it was tense. Finally, I asked why it had taken so long for me to get a meeting. Citi executives had given various justifications over the past few months. I strongly felt that discovering the reasons behind my freeze-out would give me some insight into their corporate governance shortfalls. They had told media outlets that they were not excluding me; I simply had to wait my turn. They also floated some other notions, telling the media that my firm wasn't big enough or well-known enough on Wall Street, even though it's very prominent in Asia, which Citi has identified as one of its most promising markets.

But when I asked about it now, Pandit looked down and didn't answer. One of the Citi managers indicated that this was not a topic for this meeting and that we could cover it another time. "We'll handle that later," the manager said. I then looked squarely at Pandit, reminded him of our encounter in Boston, and pressed for an answer. After a pause, he said, "Let's move forward." Realizing that I wasn't going to get an answer, I had no choice but to drop the subject.

After about an hour, the meeting was over. We all shook hands again, and my clients left happy. We had raised our concerns, Citi dismissed them, but at least I better understood their arguments, and we were all in the same room.

When I got back to the office and started to write my notes for a report I would put out for clients, I called Citi to clarify some things that had come up in the meeting. Again I brought up the issue of access—I had been told it would be discussed later, and I still hadn't gotten an answer. Why had Citi held me off for so long?

On the phone, I was given yet another reason, the most infuriating one of all. The real reason I hadn't been able to meet with management in more than two years, they said, was that they had asked institutional investors for the names of influential analysts, and my name hadn't come up. I was livid. My entire career flashed before my eyes, my 1,000-plus page research books that were critical of Citi and the industry over the prior decade, the successful calls that I made on the company even when the CEO was considered untouchable, and the difficulty I'd had of even getting a seat at the table to conduct my research in the first place. With this comment, the implication was that I simply wasn't good at my job—Citi wasn't the problem, I was. And to me, this was the final straw.

I blew up, even screaming and swearing, over the idea that after two decades on Wall Street, my work wasn't relevant.

"You take that to the CEO," I yelled, "and you tell him I said that Citi told an investor I was shut out. You take that to him!"

It was unprofessional and completely unacceptable, and it's not something I'm proud of, but it happened. I had been pushed too far.

"Mike, you're yelling," one Citi person said. "Mike, calm down."

I yelled some more, not even remembering all the things I said, and then I realized the person was right. Something a former boss of mine had said years ago came back to me now: When you talk to companies, you should always act as if the other side is recording you. They rarely are, but you should act that way, as a reminder to avoid saying something you'll regret later—which I had just done.

I calmed down. We continued on the call, getting back to the company's performance. I asked questions, they answered them. I wasn't satisfied with some of their answers, but at least they'd had a chance to give their side. And finally I hung up and started working on the report I would issue on Citi early the following week. It would take me all weekend to write.

The coup de grace was seeing that Citigroup had given a statement to the *New York Times* just a few hours after the meeting, attempting to shoot down my analysis before I'd even had a chance to publish it. Clearly, Citi was not following Pandit's directive from only a few hours earlier to "move forward." This kind of thing was unprecedented, and I'd never seen anything like it in my career.

■ ■ ■

But it didn't stop there. Four months later, the company released a new pay package for senior executives in February 2011. Citi announced the news late on the Friday afternoon before President's Day weekend—a classic strategy when companies have to disclose something but want to avoid attracting attention to it. Why try to sneak this under the radar? The bar was set ridiculously low for incentive payments. The main number that management had to hit for bonuses was cumulative pretax income of $12 billion, mostly for the "good" part of Citi, called Citicorp. (The bulk of the remainder of the company, with all the unwanted stuff, has been split off into a separate company called Citi Holdings.) That hurdle, $12 billion, may sound high, but it's about half of what the company earned in each of the last two years. As for Pandit, whose compensation terms were finalized a few months later in May, I calculated that he would make $43 million if Citi simply met consensus earnings estimates from that period, and that he would qualify for incentive compensation only a couple quarters later.

In other words, the senior team at Citi could get enormous paychecks for performance that one could quantifiably argue is merely average, including profit numbers that were lower than the company had hit over the prior two years. That is no incentive. It's like giving the manager of the Yankees a big reward for winning only half of the games in a season.

A few banks and other big companies have instituted claw-back provisions, which allow a company to recoup an executive's pay if his or her decisions lead to problems later on. Citi put in something like this, as well, though it's fairly toothless. The execs get two-thirds of their bonus amount in early 2013 and the remainder a year later (minus any losses in 2013). If any problems surface after that, there are no consequences; the executives get to keep their money. This means that if new loans or investments go bad in 2014 or later, current Citi managers could be long gone with their bonuses, just as happened during the recent crisis.

This is another way in which the company hasn't changed or learned the lessons of its history. I first highlighted the company's compensation problems back in 1999, when it got more aggressively into stock options than any other large bank. Options can be a useful tool, but they can also encourage the employees who have them to take on excessive risks in the short term, merely to move the stock price higher. And Citi's top-level pay has been seriously out of whack relative to performance. From 2000 to 2009, CEOs at Citi were paid more generously than at any other bank besides Goldman Sachs, even though Citi had by far the worst stock performance among large banks (down more than 80 percent during Pandit's tenure). That's one example of how short-term thinking aimed at pumping up asset growth and stock performance for a few quarters or a year or two can actually have the reverse effect long term.

After the compensation package drew the inevitable criticism, Dick Parsons, the current board chairman at Citi, who served on the compensation committee for the past decade and chaired it from 2002 to 2007, went on CNBC to defend the terms of Pandit's pay. Parsons noted that the CEO only earned $1 a year in 2009 and 2010. "On almost any basis," Parsons claimed, "Vikram Pandit, who's worked basically for a buck a year for the last several years, has been one of the most, if not the single most, productive employees in terms of units paid for units performed, in America."

I don't buy that, though, because Pandit made a pretty generous salary prior to his $1-a-year stint—about $38 million in 2008, along with another $165 million from the sale of his hedge fund, Old Lane Partners, to Citigroup. Old Lane is a saga in itself—Pandit launched it in 2006 and Citi bought it after its first year, during which it returned a somewhat underwhelming 6.5 percent, below average in the industry. The price was $800 million, of which Pandit's take came to $165 million.

Just a month after the deal closed, the financial crisis erupted and the fund began to lose money. It ultimately shuttered in mid-2008, due to underperformance and chronic withdrawals from investors.

In other words, while Parsons is technically correct, that argument is a bit disingenuous when you consider that during Pandit's four-year tenure at Citi, he's received more than $200 million.

Parsons had another notable statement during his CNBC appearance. "We're back in the game," Parsons said, "and a lot of that is due to Vikram and the team that he put together." But that's not fully true, either. A good part of the reason that Citi was back in the game is because of the actions of the federal government.

Once again, I have no problem with CEOs at Pandit's level making a lot of money. I just think they should have to earn it, not through intelligence or hard work or honest intentions—I'm sure Pandit qualifies on these counts—but through results over time. Sustainable growth, solid risk management, and a stock that makes money for long-term investors. And peg compensation incentives to something that feels like a legitimate achievement.

■ ■ ■

But here's the bottom line. In the current market environment, I don't think a company like Citi will ever change. Why would it? We'll continue to see changes at the margins—the CEO might leave in a few years, the company will probably reorganize itself yet again, and a new crop of people will come in telling everyone that this time things are going to be different. But that won't fundamentally alter the character of the company.

Even today, Citigroup has a big marketing campaign that talks about "the New Citi," but that's part of the problem—the company has been reinventing itself for almost 15 years, more or less nonstop since the big merger in 1998. For the record, the "New Citi" looks a lot like the old Citicorp pre-1998, before all those mergers took place. After a decade of acquisitions, the company is now trying to shed many of the assets it bought. That's a good way for investment bankers to get rich—they get paid both ways, buying and selling—but it's no way to run a bank.

What would be accomplished by letting a business like this fail someday? I don't doubt that it would involve a tremendous amount of pain, not only for investors but also for employees, customers, and everyone else who's directly involved with the company. But it would also do more than 40 years of regulation crafted on Capitol Hill or Treasury Department bailouts ever could, since it would demonstrate that risk comes with ramifications. People can debate the worthiness of programs like TARP, which many argue stabilized the U.S. financial system and minimized the damage of the real estate crisis. But there's no getting around the fact that many executives on Wall Street got tremendously wealthy by taking outsized bets for their companies and then left before those bets went bad. Some losses from the bets were socialized—picked up by the taxpayers.

My skepticism was neatly summed up by ex-FDIC head Sheila Bair, during the hectic negotiations among senior regulators back in November 2008, when they were crafting the second bailout for Citigroup. This was during the company's darkest days, and Bair was hesitant to jump in and rescue what she considered a flawed organization. "I don't think this is going to fix Citi," she said. "And unless you figure out a way to stabilize the situation, we are going to be back in here writing more checks. We all need to be realistic about some of the underlying problems at this institution. It's not just because the market is having problems; this institution has some problems very specific to itself."

Bair continued this line of thinking in a subsequent e-mail to the regulators overseeing Citi a few months later. The company, she wrote, needed "greater senior management bank experience," which meant changes "at the top of the house."

I could not agree more. Bair's concerns came out only after the crisis was over, but in hindsight, she looks increasingly right. History suggests that, just as Bair predicted, the U.S. government will be writing big checks to Citi again, probably sooner rather than later. More bailouts are on the way, for most banks on Wall Street but for Citi in particular. It's just a question of when.

My story with the bank is a little like the film *Chinatown*, where the detective played by Jack Nicholson uncovers layer after layer of corruption and crime in Los Angeles but is unable to clean it up. It's all

summed up in the famous last line of the movie, where another character turns to him and says, "Forget it, Jake. It's Chinatown." After all the
table-pounding I've done over the years, telling the world about the bad
things that Citigroup is doing, they keep getting away with it.

The truly outrageous thing about the financial crisis is not that it
happened. After all, there's a lot of money to be made on Wall Street,
and some people simply can't resist the temptation to take the fast
buck, to put their own self-interest ahead of the long-term health of
their company and of the financial system as a whole. No, the truly
outrageous thing about Citi is that all the factors that led to problems
over its long history, and especially over the past decade—questionable
accounting, the separation of risk from reward, outsized executive pay—
are *still* happening. It's like we've learned nothing. Forget it, Mike. It's
Wall Street.

Chapter 9

A Better Version of Capitalism

Not quite a decade ago, I had a curious meeting at a nondescript office in a downtown building not far from Wall Street. The person I met with was the Superintendent of the New York State Banking Department. The organization oversaw and regulated some of the biggest banks in the world. Every bank with a state charter in New York answers to this agency, and it in turn shares its information with other regulators.

The stereotype of someone in this role would be an old-school, middle-age bureaucrat with a paunch and a bad suit. In fact, the regulator was a warm and gracious mother of six and former Goldman Sachs investment banker, who thanked me for coming down to see her.

The superintendent had asked to meet with me because she wanted to hear my views about the risks in the banking sector. This was in the early 2000s, not long after the Enron disaster, WorldCom, and some other blowups after the rupture of the tech bubble. A few of the banks on Wall Street had played a key role in financing those companies, costing the banks billions of dollars in fines, settlements, and other expenses, not to mention damaging their reputations. Arthur Andersen, Enron's accountant, had gone under, and Sarbanes-Oxley would soon be put in place. It was one of those junctures—a little like the current situation in the United States—where we crawl out from under the wreckage of some financial calamity and say, "Whoa, how do we prevent that from happening again?"

I wore a freshly pressed pinstripe suit, a white shirt, and a conservative red tie to try to look important, or at least worthy of a meeting with a government official at this level. Ever since my time at the Fed, I have considered regulators a central element of the banking system, and I respect the work they do, many achieving admirable things under difficult conditions. In part, I came to the meeting hoping to see how the superintendant could use her power to help control the abuses that had recently taken place.

When I met her, we exchanged greetings and began talking. A few people from her team joined us, and I started with my main point.

"There's more risk than meets the eye at the big banks," I said. "The issue relates to commitments to lend to borrowers that have not drawn down these loans. This first got my attention when I saw a newspaper story about Xerox drawing down credit lines from banks even when the company started to have big problems."

She asked me to explain.

"Well, you had Enron in a similar situation," I said. "They drew down $3 billion from their banks only a month before they went bankrupt. I wondered how they were able to do this. It seemed strange that banks would allow this, and then I discovered that they had no choice given the terms of the loan agreements. They were locked into providing that credit."

As it turned out, the financial industry at that point had about $5 trillion in unused loan commitments that were still outstanding. The banks would often get a fee on the front end but pay the price later if the credit went bad. Earnings were front-loaded, but the risks hung around. I pointed this out as something worth looking into.

We talked for a while longer, and near the end of the conversation, she added something astonishing. Almost as an aside, while walking down the hallway, she said, "With the work you do, banks may actually listen more to you than to me, because you make their stock prices move."

I was dumbfounded. By this point in my career, I'd developed enough of a reputation that my words had some weight and, at times, could impact the stock prices of the banks I covered. But I felt that most banks weren't listening to criticism. At best, they didn't respond, at least not openly. At worst, they made overt efforts to undermine critics, by feeding selective information to more positive analysts and the media.

In other words, I was looking to her for some reassurance that regulators were on the case, and she was telling me that she thought markets were a stronger implement. It was like one of those sports bloopers where two outfielders watch a routine fly ball drop between them.

In a way, that exchange a decade ago sums up a fundamental question that has greater relevance today than perhaps at any other time in U.S. history. To fix the banking sector, should we rely more on government regulation and oversight or let the market figure it out? Tougher rules or more capitalism? Right now, we have the worst of both worlds. We have a purportedly capitalistic system with a lot of rules that are not strictly enforced, and when things go wrong, the government steps in to protect banks from the market consequences of their own worst decisions. To me, that's not capitalism.

I can understand the appeal of certain regulation. If we'd had the right oversight in place, we would have limited the degree of the financial crisis, which included bailouts measured in hundreds of billions of dollars, and millions of people losing their homes due to foreclosures. But we also would have sacrificed innovations in credit and a vibrant financial sector. Over the past century, our economy probably would not have grown as fast or been anywhere near as dynamic.

Moreover, the real problem with regulation is that it often doesn't work very well, in part because it's always considering problems in the rearview mirror. The financial system today is almost dizzyingly complex and moving at light speed, and new rules tend to address fairly precise things. They ban specific types of securities or deals or trades instead of addressing larger principles.

The Dodd-Frank Act, enacted by Congress in 2010, is a good example. Included in its roughly 2,300 pages of new legislation is a mechanism to unwind "systemically important" financial institutions. (As I write this, the banks are fighting with regulators over how the complex rules will work.) Yet regardless of that process, many believe that Wall Street banks are still too large and too interconnected, and that if they get into trouble again, the federal government will do what it's done in the past and step in to keep them in business. I recently posed this question to the audience at a conference I hosted: Are U.S. banks too big to fail? These were sophisticated investors—hedge fund managers and senior executives at financial firms, and 96 percent of them said yes. You can write all the rules and minutiae that you want, but when it comes down to it, the government can suspend those rules, or alter them, and the end result will be the same. The pain of letting one of these institutions go under is almost always too much for politicians and our government to bear.

A related issue is that regulation can sometimes trigger unintended consequences. Another section of Dodd-Frank cut the fees that a bank can charge a store for debit card transactions. As you can imagine, banks are not about to simply shrug that off. It adds up to billions each year. Instead, they'll make it up somewhere else—most likely by charging consumers for other services, as in no more free checking. The bottom line? Consumers will now pay more for the convenience of using a debit card, and will likely never see the benefits from the lower costs to merchants. This is—let's face it—price-fixing by the government, and it shows why measures like this don't really help things in the long run. If the government were to set a cap on how much McDonald's could charge for Big Macs, it wouldn't take long before the price of fries went up to cover the difference.

ATM fees are in the same category. This comes up all the time— some consumer group will start demanding that the government regulate those $2 or $3 charges that you pay when you use another company's ATM. This is irrational. The fees are completely transparent, and the bank asks you if you want to pay them, *every single time*. If not, go find another machine or become a customer at that bank. The real threat to consumers is probably the fees we don't see and are not asked about, like things buried in the fine print. Banks invest in technology all the time, and most of the projects don't pan out. The ATM is one innovation that did, a once-in-a-generation success, and so banks have every right to charge whatever the market will bear for that convenience.

I had a firsthand experience almost fifteen years ago that reminded me what life could be like without bank machines. Back in the late 1990s, Jackie and I traveled to the Galápagos Islands, and we stopped for a day in Quito, Ecuador. ATMs were not yet part of the banking system there, and on one corner in Quito we passed a bank where we saw a long line of people waiting to get their money out—literally, the line was out the door and around the building. Security guards with machine guns, the whole production. That's life without an ATM—every time you need $20 or want to cash a check, you have to wait in a line (albeit without the machine guns in the lobby). With modern technology, "going to the bank" is no longer a chore on the list with "going to the post office" and "picking up the dry cleaning."

As much as I want to believe in regulation, I think the more effective solution would come from letting market forces work. That doesn't mean no rules at all—a banking system like the Wild West, with blood on the floor and consumers being routinely swindled. Instead, I think we need a better version of capitalism. This means a cultural, perhaps *generational*, change that compels companies to better apply accounting rules based on economic substance versus surface presentation. For two decades, I've watched companies dress up their earnings with all sorts of accounting tricks, often with words such as "recapture," "release," and—one of my favorites—"reclassification." It really can be as easy as the stroke of a computer key to make more earnings materialize.

Even in 2011, some banks were woefully deficient in detailing the amount of their securities and loans that are vulnerable to the ravages of the European financial crisis. The solution is to increase transparency and let outsiders see what's really going on. This would go a long way toward at least encouraging companies to stay within the spirit of the rules. Instead of trying to control what banks do, I think we should let them off the leash but make the results more public, more transparent, and easier to understand. And we should hold banks accountable when they drop the ball.

I like to keep things simple, so the way I think of this is ABC. "A" stands for better accounting standards, to make sure that companies aren't cooking the books. "B" stands for bankruptcy, to put account- ability in the right place if companies get into trouble. And "C" stands for clout, ensuring that the deck isn't stacked in favor of insiders and against the outsiders.

■ ■ ■

ACCOUNTING

In a nutshell, all 10,000 or so publicly held companies in this country have to follow the same accounting rules, which are set by a private- sector group called the Financial Accounting Standards Board. Unfortunately, the model is based on a stale, decades-old approach, despite vast increases in corporate size and complexity. The rules require full-blown experts to understand and interpret, and there are huge gray areas, with a lot of room for creative interpretation. The result is a little like golfers deciding on their own how they're going to keep score. Unless you know what really happened out there in that sand trap on the fifth hole, the numbers they post at the end don't have much meaning, and it's almost impossible to tell who's good and who's fudging.

With all of our technology, we still can't tell for sure if the num- bers a company reports really are correct. This is what helped mask the problems at firms like Enron and WorldCom in the early 2000s, along with Lehman, Bear Stearns, Washington Mutual, Countrywide, IndyMac, Fannie Mae, Freddie Mac, and all the other companies that either folded or were sold at fire-sale prices in the past few years. On paper, these companies all received a clean bill of health right up until the end. Any problems were hidden inside their financial statements, like mystery meat passed off as USDA prime steak.

The biggest threat to the financial system is one we probably don't know about yet. It's out there right now, lurking like a spore colony, tucked in some hidden crevice in the finances of big banks but not yet disclosed to investors. Given that most of these companies have very complex transactions and business structures, and billions of dollars hinging on how those arrangements are accounted for, some tougher standards would go a long way toward eliminating the gray areas and giving investors a clear idea of how each company is actually performing compared to its peers.

For example, in 2009, a big bank raised eyebrows when it transferred a large amount of mortgage securities from one accounting category that pegged them at current market values to another category that did so at the original full price. Then, in 2011, as values for those securities started trending upward, it moved a portion of the securities back and realized a profit as a result. This was not illegal, but it showed the high degree of discretion that banks have in how they record the value of their assets.

Similarly, Lehman deployed a notorious strategy using dodgy accounting—called "repo 105." This complex approach more or less allowed the company to move assets off the balance sheet at the end of every quarter and then buy them back a few days into the next quarter. As a result, its books looked significantly better than they really were—about $50 billion in artificial improvements, sheer window dressing—in the months before Lehman failed in September 2008.

Small banks can be just as creative. A regional bank called Wilmington Trust was sold in November 2010, and as part of the due diligence, the acquirer (M&T Bank) went through its entire loan portfolio. In just eleven days of legwork—eleven days!—M&T realized that the problem loans on the books at Wilmington Trust were about 50 percent worse than the company had disclosed. As a result, Wilmington was worth far less than prior accounting values would have indicated. In fact, its book value was cut in half, not exactly a rounding error.

These are extreme examples but definitely not isolated events. My estimates in mid 2011 were that banks still sat on about $300 billion in losses due to problem assets from the financial crisis that don't show up because of leeway in accounting rules.

Two key principles would help. First, financial statements should reflect the substance of a transaction rather than merely the legal mechanics. For example, Lehman's repo 105 deals weren't intended to permanently change the ownership of the securities. Instead, they were merely to get the books to look a certain way. The accounting field used to have a rule preventing this kind of window-dressing, but it was repealed back in 1993. While standards have been updated to prevent specific situations like the one at Lehman, I'd argue for broader reform, to make the accounting treatment of transactions like this show what's really going on.

Second, given that the rule makers can't possibly write enough rules to cover every potential transaction, a single broad principle should go into effect saying that banks must disclose material information. There's no single precise definition of "material"—it means anything that would significantly impact the company's financials. But under the current rules, management can simply decline to mention some major stuff.

For example, most big banks today face a lot of current and potential lawsuits related to the mortgages that they originated and then sold to others. Yet the banks don't have to record all of the potential costs of those loans—including legal expenses, settlements, and jury awards—until they're pretty sure the costs are really coming and can predict the amount fairly accurately. As a result, these costs don't show up until very late in the process.

Auditors are another big part of the problem. These are the firms that sign off on the banks' internal accounting. There are only four main audit and accounting firms, down from the so-called Big Eight of the 1990s—KPMG, Ernst & Young, Deloitte Touche Tohmatsu, and PwC (formerly known as Pricewaterhouse Coopers)—and they're supposed to bring third-party objectivity to the accounting process. Yet auditors have a knack for saying that everything is OK, even when it might not be. That stems from an inherent conflict of interest, in that auditors are hired, fired, and paid directly by the company they're evaluating. Specifically, they're brought in by the audit committee, which is a subset of the board of directors.

These audits are extremely large projects, resulting in massive fees. Bank of America (BofA), for example, paid audit and related fees of $107 million in 2010, plus another $16 million in tax accounting fees. The process often involves 100,000 to 400,000 man-hours spent poring through the company's books, and the result of all that time and effort is somewhat underwhelming: three or four boilerplate paragraphs that are almost always the same as in the prior year, and the same for 95 percent of all companies. That's a lot of time and expense for a brief statement in dense legalese, complete gobbledygook. In the case of BofA, that amounted to 568 words, or $188,000 per word. Auditing operates on a pass/fail model, where just about all companies pass every year. Enron passed. Lehman passed. Wilmington Trust passed. Pass/fail may be a rational approach for first-semester college freshmen, but large financial institutions deserve a more nuanced grading system.

Because of these substantial fees, many auditing firms develop long-standing relationships with the companies they audit. Citigroup has changed its name multiple times in the past forty-one years, but it still has the same auditor, KPMG. That relationship probably exceeds the tenure of just about every single employee at both companies.

In the wake of Enron—and Arthur Andersen's failure to spot problems within the company—the Sarbanes-Oxley Act of 2002 created a new group called the Public Company Accounting Oversight Board (PCAOB) specifically to oversee the auditors and the Big Four accounting firms. It's a nonprofit organization, and for most of its existence thus far, it has tried to get its arms around the problem. Its conclusions have not been pretty.

Of 2,800 auditor/client relationships that the PCAOB reviewed, it found hundreds of failures. In one case, an auditor realized that a company it was reviewing had overstated its earnings but avoided a correction by—ready for this?—increasing the tolerance for misstatements by 50 percent. If the number doesn't fall within your parameters, change the parameters! The company had been a client of the auditing firm for ninety-eight years.

To improve the process, I'd argue that those hundreds of thousands of hours that auditors spend with a company should lead to more actionable information. Some of that information could go directly to shareholders—who, after all, are the people who actually own the company. Rather than being a simple pass/fail designation, audit results could include more details and conclusions, with a descriptive section about possible risks or anything else that might keep an auditor awake at night. The point would be to spread knowledge and let all investors and potential investors see exactly what the auditors found.

There are other solutions, as well. One would be to require that companies change their auditor on some periodic basis, such as every ten years. Because these are complex companies, there's a learning curve for auditors and a company expense to switching them, but a decade seems reasonable to me. Another option is to have the lead partner of the audit sign his or her name to the report instead of merely the firm's name. People in other professions put their names on their work, such as lawyers, doctors, analysts, and journalists, which fosters greater accountability. Indeed, bank CEOs and CFOs must now attest to the accuracy of the financial statements—one of the best parts of Sarbanes-Oxley—though there is still plenty of wiggle room for aggressive accounting. These changes have been proposed by the PCAOB; predictably, though, the audit companies are balking.

Regardless of which of these measures get implemented, the ultimate goal should be to increase transparency, so that everyone—investors, analysts, journalists, and any other stakeholders—can keep score accurately and compare companies consistently. It's as basic as having confidence in the numbers and making sure that the books aren't cooked. Almost a hundred years ago, Supreme Court Justice Louis Brandeis described the benefits of openness and transparency. "Sunlight," he wrote, "is said to be the best of disinfectants." To that I'd add: "Let the sun shine in."

■ ■ ■

BANKRUPTCY

I was out with my son in 2009 when we saw a hand-lettered sign in a shop that said "Deadbeats will not be tolerated." He asked me what a deadbeat was.

"It's someone who doesn't pay his bills," I explained.

"Like the banking crisis," my son responded.

I don't know how he made this connection. He was seven at the time, and I try to avoid talking about my job when I'm home. But the topic was ubiquitous, and he must have absorbed something that he had heard. I explained that some customers—like some banks and borrowers during the crisis—did not always pay their bills, and that "deadbeat" was the old-fashioned way to refer to these people.

We let the conversation drop there, but it must have stayed on his mind. During the school year, he had an assignment in his class to write a letter to the president, on a topic of his choice, and he wrote this (I corrected his misspellings):

Dear Mr. President:
I voted for you. My dad is a bank analyst. I came up with an idea for banks failing. My idea is to make a law saying that everyone has to pay their bills or else they have to go to trial. I love you. I hope you will make peace. Good luck.

He also included a peace sign, which I thought was a nice touch.

I told him that there are mitigating circumstances in some cases and that we have a duty to help the truly poor. But I was struck by how the solution to the banking crisis was clear even to a seven-year-old: People or companies that don't pay their bills have to be held accountable.

To me, there should be no such thing as "too big to fail." Banks that get into trouble should be allowed to go under. In fact, I'm not sure that size is even the key issue here. Banks have become massive over the past generation—the five largest U.S. banks in 2011 control two-thirds of the industry based on their size, which is a greater degree of consolidation than before the crisis. Some of these banks have increased in size twentyfold over the two decades that I've been working on Wall Street, and three of them each now have about $2 trillion in assets, making them bigger than many national economies. If it's size that we're worried about, we're already too late.

Incidentally, two things are worth noting about these super-size banks. First, much of their growth has come from mergers and acquisitions. They're not growing like Google, by creating a product and doing it better than anyone else. Instead, they're just buying out their competitors. That can be OK if it means more efficient banks but not if they get so big that they can't be managed well. Second, many of these banks would likely not have grown to their current size without federal assistance in the past. In all the bank crises of previous decades, bank failures were thought to be too economically disruptive. But government bailouts—including the most recent round—didn't resolve that problem. They merely delayed it, allowing banks to keep growing in size and scope, making the potential cataclysm next time that much bigger.

The real question isn't size but execution. Some big companies operate very well without outside intervention. The ones that don't should go away. I realize that this process would involve pain, but the collapse of a single massive bank would do more than just about any regulation you could write up, because it would remind everyone of the definition of risk. In fact, bankruptcy isn't some aberrant condition—it's a crucial part of the capitalist system, summed up by the phrase "creative destruction." The failure of the weakest allows the strong to survive. By contrast, consider Japan and its zombie banks and companies, propped up by years of failed government policies.

In the current U.S. system, the potential gain from risky behaviors on Wall Street far outweighs the potential loss if things go wrong. You can get rich, and if it doesn't work out . . . you can try getting rich again. Given the widespread damage that some banking ventures have caused to the country's overall economy lately, failure needs to carry consequences, and those consequences should be steep. (Warren Buffett said something along these lines recently. If he were in charge of the nation's economy and a bank were to fail, he said, "The CEO and his [family] would forfeit their net worth.")

Some might point to the failure of Lehman as evidence that allowing failures still does not change much about Wall Street. But Lehman was the exception that proves the rule. The government deliberately let that happen—it made a conscious decision not to help—and that decision was considered a surprise at the time. However, the next time a bank ran into problems, a few months later, the government stepped back in with a bailout for the entire sector. It didn't establish a precedent about failure and consequences—it merely deviated one time from its usual policy, after much deliberation, and returned to it immediately afterward.

At a minimum, large banks that experience serial mishaps should be broken up and sold off in pieces—a middle ground between the current situation, where the government serves as a backstop, and complete bankruptcy. This kind of measure might be tough to execute, but share-holders would probably benefit. In my view, companies in trouble are usually worth more as separate divisions than they are bundled into one problematic whole.

Fundamentally, the reason that banks need to feel the consequences of their actions is because typically they're not meant to be growth stocks. They're not supposed to grow at warp speed or somehow dis-cover a loophole in the basic rules of finance. For a while, some new idea or asset class will show promise, but then everyone will pile in, inflate the value, and suffer horribly when it inevitably collapses. Banks shouldn't work like that, yet many of them did. They chased growth, and they made unwise moves to generate it.

If you want a model for how banks should operate—not only avoiding risky behaviors, and bankruptcy, but also delivering returns to shareholders—consider an unlikely candidate: M&T Bank. It's a regional player based in Buffalo, New York, the twenty-first largest bank in the country. The name stands for Manufacturers and Traders, a leftover from its nineteenth-century origins. M&T has about 800 branches throughout the Northeast and Mid Atlantic, and in terms of operations, it's fairly boring. No financial engineering, no expansion into emerging markets. However here's the really important number: Since 1983, M&T has been the best-performing large bank stock.

That kind of slow, steady return comes from focusing on avoiding losses, minimizing risk, and not chasing growth. M&T limits its fool-ish mistakes, and it doesn't get caught up in financial fads. It also helps that the bank avoids management turnover—the current CEO has been in place since the early 1980s—and it does not pay its executives exorbitantly. Top-level managers get about a tenth of the compensa-tion as those at other banks and own about ten times more stock in their bank. When asked about the low-growth, low-risk, and low-pay approach, the company responds simply: "That's the way we operate around here."

This is the lesson for banks on how to run their companies. If you drive 60 mph in a 30 mph zone, you'll have accidents. If you drive within the speed limit, you'll stay safe, and over the long run, you'll likely end up ahead. Given that the United States is likely to have slow growth rates closer to what the city of Buffalo has seen, I wish I could say that more banks would operate like M&T and stick with a conservative approach. Instead, I'm pretty sure that many of them will try to dream up creative ways to spur growth—they'll sacrifice long-term success by chasing short-term gains. And they will possibly threaten the viability of their company, and taint the entire financial system, by doing so.

CLOUT

The final letter, C, stands for clout. Bank executives today hold tremendous power, and the entities and individuals that are supposed to serve as a check on their actions—boards of directors, analysts, regulators, and others—either get co-opted or shouted down. I'd argue that we need to redirect some of the clout away from banks and insiders and more toward outsiders so they can take an objective or even adversarial stance.

Let's start with boards of directors. Boards are typically responsible for three things: (1) hiring a CEO and evaluating that person's compensation and performance; (2) setting an overall risk appetite at the bank; and (3) providing the company with some kind of independent oversight. In all three areas, boards have struck out lately, yet in most cases they remain largely intact and unchanged.

Compensation has been a problem for more than a decade. I first raised this as a serious issue in 1998, when I was vocal in my criticism that banks relied too much on stock options and that bank CEOs in particular were paid too much, a trend that has only accelerated since that time. In very round numbers, the paychecks of bank CEOs at the largest banks have increased from six figures in the 1980s to seven figures in the 1990s and eight figures in the 2000s. This pay has little correlation with performance, and the crisis was little more than a blip in that escalation. If you run a well-organized financial entity that doesn't require bailouts or take on excessive risk, and if you can consistently increase earnings and generate high returns for investors, you should claim whatever salary and bonus the market will support. But conversely, if things go wrong, you shouldn't get to walk away with the fat paycheck anyway.

Boards of directors are the people who sign off on these decisions, and all too frequently boards are stuffed with insiders: CEOs and former CEOs, rich people who travel in different circles from the rest of the world.

Even worse, sometimes directors have little understanding of the company's operations, which pretty much rules out the chance that they might spot potential problems. McKinsey & Company, the consulting firm, recently published the results of a survey of corporate board members that backs this up. The survey was in 2011, three years after the crisis, when a lack of board oversight was considered one of the key factors. Yet only 21 percent of the directors who responded said they had a complete understanding of the company's strategy. In the financial sector, the number was even worse: Just 6 percent claimed to fully grasp the operating strategy. That's astounding to me.

The survey also asked board members specific ways that they could get better. Most respondents thought that they needed to spend more time on company business, with access to better and more timely information. They also thought that a better range of backgrounds and expertise levels among board members would help. While these organizations are certainly better off with experienced professionals, there's also a lot of room for diverse viewpoints, which would bring some needed objectivity to the process.

■ ■ ■

Analysts are supposed to be another check on the financial system—people like me, who can wade through a company's financials and tell investors what's really going on. There are about 5,000 so-called sell-side analysts, about 5 percent of whom track the financial sector, serving as watchdogs over U.S. companies with combined market value of more than $15 trillion. (The other side of equity research consists of buy-side analysts, who work directly for firms like hedge funds, mutual fund companies, and other investment companies; their analyses and ratings typically aren't made public.)

Yet as a whole, we need to do better, which is a challenge because there simply aren't enough effective analysts to hold companies accountable. Of the group of sell-side analysts tracking a specific company, a handful will be new, without enough experience or scope to identify problems, and another group will be little more than cheerleaders. The proportion of sell ratings on Wall Street remains only 5 percent, even today, yet any first-year MBA student can tell you that

95 percent of the stocks cannot be winners. I hear these perma-bull analysts all the time on quarterly earnings calls. They get called on first to ask their softball questions, and they sometimes begin by saying something like, "Good quarter," as if they're congratulating the CEO for doing his job.

Not surprisingly, my questions don't always get taken on earnings calls. Banks sometimes just don't want to hear my questions, especially when other analysts are listening in. Sometimes the companies simply ignore me—after all, these are conference calls, and management can shape the conversation by limiting which questions get asked. One recent study by the National Investor Relations Institute found that 80 percent of companies—not just banks but all public companies— screen questions during earnings calls, without disclosing that they're doing so. I'm still surprised when this happens: I'm dialed into the call and pushing the correct button on the keypad until my finger goes numb, yet my questions might not get taken. Management will announce that they're out of time, as if there's something more important than addressing the concerns of shareholders—the people who own the company—and analysts like me who look after their interests.

When I am allowed a question—often near the end of the call— sometimes I ask something so stunningly obvious that I can't believe it hasn't come up sooner. In January 2011, BofA held an earnings call to talk about its financial results, and it included an important disclosure. The company was involved in multiple lawsuits relating to mortgages that the company originated. (BofA acquired Countrywide in early 2008, one of the biggest originators of the subprime loans that led to the housing crisis.) During the call, the company said that the upper limit of its exposure from those lawsuits would be $7 billion to $10 billion. Other analysts jumped in to discuss other aspects of the financials, some fairly arcane and technical. I finally got called on—as the eighth analyst after twenty-eight prior questions during that call. My question: Was that $7 billion to $10 billion before tax or after tax? The answer meant a swing of approximately $3 billion in the company's financials. Incidentally, BofA's estimate was before tax, though within a few months the company had already exceeded the bounds it cited on that call.

Sometimes I get a less than friendly response to my questions. In 2011, KeyCorp announced that it had pulled so much money out of its reserves against bad loans that it was able to report a gain in this line item. Even in the slightly unreal world of accounting, this was an extremely aggressive move, since reserves are almost always treated as an expense item. KeyCorp's move was like someone pulling money out of his savings account and claiming he just got a raise. I asked about it during the earnings call and whether this unconventional maneuver helped bolster compensation. The CEO responded that he found my question "a bit offensive." To be clear, I'm not sure about the degree of any link—banks aren't required to tell us if there is—and if one existed, it might be minor. But I should at least be allowed to ask the question. One investor who heard my question on the conference call later e-mailed me to say "I found the CEO's response to your question offensive."

At other times, companies simply refuse to disclose critical information. In July 2011, Capital One announced its quarterly earnings, along with a $2 billion equity offering to help pay off an acquisition. This was a significant transaction, but the company declined to hold its typical quarterly call and in fact disclosed *less* information than in a standard earnings release. In particular, it omitted the profit-and-loss summary for its different business segments—critical information if you want to understand the company's current situation, growth prospects, and any weaknesses. When analysts asked, the bank rebuffed the questions until after the new equity had been sold. It was like selling a car without letting buyers test-drive it—or even open the hood. As it turned out, the financial details that were later released showed a lower yield on the company's core credit card portfolio, which normally would draw tough scrutiny. Yet Capital One released the new information at 5:13 P.M. on a Friday in August, when most of the financial sector was already gone for the weekend. Investors who had purchased stock from the offering a month earlier were already underwater.

Goldman Sachs, even with an effort to improve its disclosure starting in 2011, still showed 30 percent of its total revenues—from one trading area known as fixed income, currencies and commodities— as a *single number*. The financial statements did not give much helpful underlying information, no trends to consider or data on how much each component contributed to this line item. Despite notable progress, Goldman still had an information void, a black box that investors were asked to take on faith. That's not winning the game—it's throwing sand in the ref's eyes.

■ ■ ■

The third group of outsiders with insufficient clout are regulators. As much respect as I have for the role of regulators, they simply can't oversee banks with sufficient scrutiny. For one thing, they're vastly outnumbered, outspent, and outgunned by Wall Street. While regulators will never be able to compete in terms of spending or staff numbers, the United States may want to look to London for ideas. In the last decade, the U.K. equivalent of the Securities Exchange Commission (called the Financial Services Authority) fired much of its staff and hired back higher-caliber talent, at higher salaries. This reduced the motivation for regulators to jump to more lucrative private sector jobs and improved the understanding between banks and regulators.

In the United States, the two primary regulators—the Federal Reserve and the Treasury Department—essentially have a revolving door that allows senior bank executives to jump between the public and private sectors. Henry Paulson, a Goldman CEO, was Treasury Secretary under George W. Bush. The person who Paulson replaced at Treasury, John Snow, now heads the board of private equity firm Cerberus Capital Management. Even Alan Greenspan now serves as a consultant to Pimco, an investment firm that specializes in bonds. The list goes on.

This flow of senior executives between the public and private sectors only fosters an insider culture in which those with access and clout get to make the rules, particularly through lobbying to weaken any laws that might impact their business. For the decade leading up to the financial crisis, the finance industry spent $2.7 billion on lobbying efforts, and it continues to spend at close to record levels today. A recent study by the National Bureau of Economic Research found a direct correlation between lobbying by lenders and a decrease in regulation. From 1999 to 2006, 93 percent of the bills that attempted to tighten lending regulations were shot down before they could become law.

If U.S. regulators wanted to act tough, they could have taken a much stronger stance after the financial crisis. In fact, they could have said that they "will not waver in [our] desire to ensure that public confidence in the . . . banking system is maintained through appropriate disclosure and reinvigoration of its policy of zero tolerance on all professional and unethical conduct." Or they could have said that they will "ensure that officers of banks and debtors who contribute to bank failures are brought to book to the full extent of the law and that all proceeds of infractions are confiscated where legally feasible."

However, these statements didn't come from U.S. Fed chairman Ben Bernanke but from the head of the Central Bank of Nigeria, after that country's banking crisis in 2009. Should executives who make honest mistakes in running their businesses be thrown in jail? Probably not, but this is the kind of statement that sets a strong tone from the top. Who would have thought that the U.S. banking system would cede the ethical high ground to Nigeria?

■ ■ ■

In this debate between regulation and market forces, it's been interesting to see positions evolve over time. In 1997, Alan Greenspan, then chairman of the Federal, said, "No market is ever truly unregulated. The self-interest of market participants generates private market regulation." He meant that analysts and investors were sufficient to keep banks in line and that the government should more or less stay out. A decade later, during withering questioning before a congressional committee hearing in 2008, he conceded that he was wrong on this. I don't think he was truly wrong, though. It's not that capitalism doesn't work—it does, provided there's enough transparency and sufficient information for everyone to see and understand what's really going on.

The government should protect consumers, but I don't think it can—or should—micromanage free market behavior. A couple of decades ago, if a consumer borrowed too much money and went broke, it was his fault and both the bank and the borrower had to suffer the consequences. Today, the overleveraged borrower is a victim, the bank is blamed for making the loan, and we all pay through government bailouts.

Instead, we need a better version of capitalism. That version starts with accounting: Let banks operate with a lot of latitude, but make sure outsiders can see the numbers (the *real* numbers). It also includes

bankruptcy: Let those who stand to gain from the risks they take—
lenders, borrowers, and bank executives—also remain accountable for
mistakes. And a better version of capitalism means a reduction in the
clout of big banks. All of the third-party entities that oversee them
need sufficient latitude to serve as a true check and balance. My peer
group, the army of 5,000 sell-side Wall Street analysts, can help lead
the way to provide scrutiny over the markets. Doing this involves a
culture change to ensure that analysts can act with sufficient intellec-
tual curiosity and independence to critically analyze public companies
that control so much of our economy.

These steps are as simple as ABC, but they would go a long way in
helping to ensure the banking sector creates the lasting value that has
been so elusive in recent years.

Chapter 10

The Meaning of Life

There's a great scene in *Den of Thieves*, the definitive book about Wall Street's insider trading scandals of the 1980s, in which Ivan Boesky dines out. Boesky was one of the central villains in that book—he made himself rich by cultivating relationships that would give him advance notice of mergers, which allowed him to buy up positions before those deals were announced. It's an effective strategy, and it's also illegal. Boesky pleaded guilty, helped investigators prosecute Michael Milken, and served a couple of years in prison.

In this scene, while he's at the height of his powers, Boesky is at Café des Artistes, which at the time was a temple of fine dining just off Central Park West in Manhattan. Boesky can't decide what he wants, so he simply doesn't decide. He orders every single entrée on the menu, and the waiter rolls out a cart with eight plates. After tasting each entrée, Boesky picks his favorite and sends the rest back. He pays for them all but eats only one.

For a short while, I did a less extravagant version of this, not at an upscale Manhattan restaurant but at an old-fashioned luncheonette. When my two older kids were four and two, I would sometimes take them to breakfast, partly to demonstrate that I was capable of handling this venture alone. During the summer, we would go to a place on the east end of Long Island called Bun and Burger. It's the standard setup—old-fashioned milk shakes, seven blue-cushioned booths, and about a dozen or so swivel seats at the counter. Signs hang down from the ceiling to announce "Please wait for the waitress to seat you" and "Sorry no single persons seated at booths."

Amid this no-frills atmosphere, my approach to feeding my kids was comically extravagant. I thought that my daughter would eat a cheese omelet, but I wasn't sure, so I also ordered French toast for her. My son usually ate oatmeal as long as I ordered extra brown sugar, but just in case, I got him raisin pancakes, too. Sometimes they liked hard-boiled eggs, so I ordered a couple of those. For insurance, I got sides of sausage and hash browns, plus muffins (blueberry and corn, toasted). It felt like I ordered the entire menu, and when food arrived, the waitress had a hard time fitting all the plates on the table.

My rationale was that I didn't want to leave and find out later that my kids were still hungry, meaning I hadn't done my job. But after a few weekend mornings of this routine, I realized that it might not be the best approach. I was spoiling and confusing my kids by giving them too many choices, not to mention wasting a ton of food. Even though I was doing one job—getting them fed—I was not doing another, which is to teach them to appreciate what they have.

On the whole, I've increasingly taken this as my perspective over the years: Money can accomplish a lot of things, but it's not going to get you off the hook for the challenges and problems of life. It's not inherently good or bad—it's a tool, nothing more. But when money is put ahead of other considerations, including professional scruples, things can go wrong.

■ ■ ■

My big negative call on the banking sector back in 1999 caused such a stir because most analysts were positive at the time, in banking and just about every other sector, and by the somewhat skewed rules of Wall Street, being positive made sense. You could get rich by putting out positive ratings, especially in the bull market of the late 1990s. My negative call went against that thinking, and a lot of people couldn't understand why I'd take such a stance. After all, the culture of free market capitalism assumes that people have an unlimited desire for material goods. I was putting all that aside and betting my career on a principle—my right to say, truthfully, what I really thought about the banks I covered—and that made others suspicious. They thought I must have had some ulterior motive, some angle I was playing, which they couldn't figure out. My angle was that, at this specific moment in time, I wanted to exercise my free will to do my job as I saw fit: to speak truthfully about the problems I saw in the banking sector, with no regrets in the process.

This was a big risk, one that could have potentially derailed or ended my career. I'd seen this happen to others. One analyst in 1990 said that the Trump organization's new Atlantic City casino, the Taj Mahal, wouldn't make it "once the cold winds blow from October to February." I would remember the quote a decade later, when I was about to make my call, given the injustice—he was fired for making these comments and later was proven correct.

But I was willing to take the chance. I'm not sure if this stemmed from anything that I was taught, but it could have been a reaction to how I was raised. I come from a solidly middle-class background. When my stepdad had his aluminum siding business, a few times he needed to bail out workers from jail so that they could show up on Monday (and finish the jobs he had promised would be done). A lot of my relatives didn't go to college, or they started but didn't make it through. My siblings and I never had any sense of entitlement growing up. If I'd had to sacrifice my Wall Street career and return to that kind of existence, it wouldn't have been the end of the world.

I have a specific recollection of visiting my stepdad and mom's restaurant, Vagabond, in Bethesda. I used to drop by some nights while I was in high school, at the time of night when the place was transitioning from the drinking crowd at the bar to the diners at their tables. My stepdad was in his element, talking to everyone, joking with customers, marshaling the busboys before the dinner rush. On this particular night I came in around six and he gave me a big hug, then nodded in the direction of a man at the end of the bar. "See that guy there?" I looked over casually. "That guy's a millionaire. He built a lot of Bethesda," my stepdad said. "And he's a schmuck."

Now he had my attention. I had never seen a millionaire in person before. I remember thinking, How can someone be so successful and still be a schmuck?

My stepdad took a sip of his drink and said, "He has all this money and he keeps working trying to make more. He doesn't know how to enjoy himself. He should just quit now and go have some fun."

That was a vivid memory—a millionaire, presented by a man I respected, as someone not taking pleasure in life. For years after that, I thought the way my stepdad did. You work to make money, and once you've made enough, you stop. But now I'm certain that that attitude is, at best, an oversimplification.

When I was just out of college in 1985, I played blackjack for a while. This was an unsettled period in my life. Some of my friends were still having fun going to parties at the University of Maryland, while others were starting careers that they felt passionately about or going to graduate school to get business or law degrees. I was working at IBM and wasn't at all sure what I'd do with my life, beyond a growing sense that it would not involve working at IBM. Some nights, I went with a friend to mini-casinos that were held at Prince Georges County firehouses, not far from my old campus in College Park. As long as you were gambling, they gave you free food—turkey sandwiches and the like—and free draft beer. Those are two very strong selling points when you're twenty-two.

I'd read a few books on blackjack and learned when to split cards and when to double down. Strategies like these were restricted at the firehouse games, but Atlantic City was a four-hour drive away, so we took a trip there, as well. I turned out to be decent at the game, to the point where I actually thought about devoting myself to further effort. I figured I could teach myself to count cards, which would put the odds more decisively in my favor. At the time, it seemed like I could make more doing that than working 9 to 5.

But even if that assumption was right—probably a long shot—after a little more thought, I was less convinced about this as a worthwhile endeavor. If I won, I'd only want to win more the next time. If I lost, I'd want to keep going and make it back. Moreover, what would I be accomplishing, just sitting around all day in casinos? There was no meaning in what I'd be doing, just free food—which was definitely not free on the nights when I lost—and a quick thrill, which proved to be fleeting. Luckily, I got accepted into an MBA program, which forced me to start spending my time more wisely.

Years later, when I was fired in 2000 and again had excess time on my hands, I started to ask the same questions. Credit Suisse had called my bluff—I made my big call, and I lost my job because of it. And I quickly realized that money wasn't the issue. I was miserable. You can play only so much golf. I felt like the world had stopped, and I was just hanging around, taking naps on the couch every afternoon instead of doing the work I loved. Pretty quickly I started to wonder why my existence mattered. What difference was I making in the world? It really hit me that life without purpose is an empty existence.

This was a glimpse of what life would be like if I actually got to the Number—if I could even calculate the Number—and it showed the problem with that thinking: It's all about the finish line and not the race. Some people can be content lying on the beach indefinitely, but I can't. I desperately wanted to keep working. Maybe that millionaire at the Vagabond stayed at his job because he enjoyed it. Clearly, he was good at it, and perhaps he drew a sense of meaning from going into the office every day and achieving something. Solving problems, seeing a piece of land improve and become someone's home or business.

In an indirect way, my stepdad would give me another lesson about money. Throughout his life, he went through a series of financial problems, to the point where he had to declare personal bankruptcy after the restaurant closed. Because he and I shared the same first and last name, after he died I got calls intended for him from collection agencies. Once it happened during a baby-naming ceremony for our youngest daughter, when our home was filled with friends and family. I always explained that there were two different Mike Mayos and that I wasn't the one they wanted, and they could establish this by checking Social Security numbers. These efforts didn't always succeed in clearing my name—I've been rejected for a few credit cards because of this confusion. The entire situation is somewhat embarrassing for me—it's a continual reminder of why money is a complex topic and why I need to be prepared for a financial setback at any time.

■ ■ ■

My joy comes from being good at my job, not buying stuff. The process of shopping, even for luxurious things, isn't at all enjoyable to me. At times, in fact, it's been deeply unpleasant. When we renovated our home, Jackie handled all the design decisions, but because we were putting in a home office for me, I had a single task—select a chair for that office. I had to meet the designer at the D&D Building at 59th and Third Avenue in New York. The name stands for Design and Decorating, and the building is a collection of stores that sell directly to "the trade," meaning to professional designers and architects only. I had no idea that such a place existed.

We entered what seemed to be a football field–size showroom with rows and rows of display areas. I saw soft chairs and hard chairs, wing chairs, club chairs, Louis XIV chairs, and chairs that probably have no name. Some had ottomans and others didn't, though of course ottomans were sold individually, so if your chair didn't come with one, you could find a match. After five minutes, I told the designer I didn't think I could last much longer.

There was more. Some chairs had strips of cloth around the base, called "skirts," which meant another array of options: shirred shirt, tall skirt, kick-pleat skirt, waterfall skirt, and the plain old standard skirt (nine inches). I was getting dizzy.

Then there was the back of the chair, which could be open, tight back, boxed, variable pitch, semiattached, button, tufted, or nailhead. Finishes could be mahogany, burnt mahogany, dark mahogany, purmiced chestnut, ebony, drift pine, and honey walnut, plus custom finishes, of course. There was bullion fringe, upholstered tapered legs, fitted side panels, optional pillows, full-pitch recliners . . . and none of this even addressed the color or texture of the fabric, meaning another few thousand options to sift through.

I finally couldn't take it anymore and left for the gym, huffing "I just want a chair!"

I thought, Is this what the extra work was about all these years? Is this why I worked until midnight, took red-eye flights to Europe, got stuck in office waiting rooms and hotels, why I got mocked by CEOs and shunned by colleagues? All so I could buy a chair? Was that really the reward? I would rather just stand.

This is another way in which Paul Volcker, the former Fed chairman, is my role model: his attitude about money. Volcker was the original Man of Silver. I recently heard an anecdote about him, when some people were bragging about a hotshot young hedge fund manager and how that person had done extremely well in a given year. Volcker took this in, thought for a moment, and said, "I have something that he'll never have: enough."

■ ■ ■

I learned another lesson during my time in exile, after I was fired in 2000: Children can help you stay focused on what's important, too. During that six-month period, I spent a lot of time with our newborn daughter, which was a completely new experience for me. In the years since then, I've tried to keep this balance—I don't always succeed, but by shuffling my schedule, I've been able to stay involved in my kids' lives. Occasionally, for example, I schedule work dinners at 8:00 P.M. or later, so I can go home for a few hours, see my kids before they go to bed, and then go back out to meet with clients. When I explain why, just about everyone understands.

At times, the juxtaposition of these two worlds can be jarring. Once, after returning from a business trip of several days, I took time off midday to take my daughter to an exhibit of butterflies at the Museum of Natural History on the Upper West Side of Manhattan. The exhibit was in a warm, humidified chamber on the ground floor, which made it feel like the tropics. Shortly before we went in, I got a cell phone call from someone quizzing me on why JPMorgan's stock was increasing that day, particularly since I had said that the stock should go down. It was a miniature short squeeze, and because I was the only analyst with a negative stance, I was more wrong than anyone else that day. I answered the question quickly and moved inside to look at butterflies, unsure about whether I was sweating more due to the heated room or the phone call.

Another day I remember attending a conference on a large merger in the morning, meeting with a bank CEO midday, and leaving work at 3:30 to attend music class in the late afternoon, where I bounced my two-year-old son up and down on a red ball while singing goofy songs. ("I am a bouncing ball, I bounce without a fall . . .") The music teacher announced to the class that she had seen "Sam's daddy" on television. A few years later, I was at a similar class with my youngest daughter when my BlackBerry went off and I absolutely had to take the call. This was during 2007, when we were getting the first inkling of how bad the financial crisis might really be. "I'll be right back!" I called brightly over my shoulder, racing out. In the lobby, I talked with someone in my office about the billions of dollars of risky assets that a bank had just disclosed. On the other side of the glass divide, the teacher was waving hand puppets around and singing to a room filled with kids, one of them mine, all of them blissfully unaware of what was happening a few miles south on Wall Street.

■ ■ ■

My wife is a doctor, and between the two of us, you'd think that she would be the one who derives more of a sense of purpose from her work. She is an internist and consults with patients before they are admitted for surgery, evaluating their medical histories and making sure that it will be safe to go ahead with the procedure. Sometimes the patients are anxious or scared, and every once in a while she'll catch something serious and previously undiagnosed. In other words, from my perspective, she directly improves and maybe even saves lives. She loves her career, and she finds meaning in the enjoyment of her work and the sense of order and security that she provides to people at a vulnerable moment in their lives.

But she doesn't think the meaning of life comes from work, even in a profession like medicine. Perhaps this is because her work is inherently imbued with human contact and meaning. She's not constantly confronted with questions of money and the existential abyss it can create. My wife is a scientist and a pragmatist, and she argues that there really isn't an overall meaning to life at all. We're programmed by our biological makeup to survive and reproduce, and that's it. It's a very human impulse to think there should be some meaning to our existence, but she can maintain enough distance to argue that there isn't necessarily one at all. I think this is also why she's so good at the spousal function of keeping my head on straight. On certain days when I've accomplished something major at work, she hugs me when I tell her about it and says, "Great job. Now go take out the trash."

It's ironic—the Wall Street guy arguing about passion and meaning in his work, and his wife, the doctor, saying no, it's a myth, end of story. But I really believe my side of this dispute. I think the meaning of life is to find something you're good at, something you love, and work to make that situation just a little bit better than it would have been without you. There's a phrase in Judaism, *tikkun olam*, which means "repairing the world." The concept is that people shouldn't do something simply because the religion requires it but rather because it makes things—something, *anything*—a little bit better.

I recognize that many on Wall Street do not look to their jobs for any greater meaning than if they made money at the blackjack table. While that doesn't work for me, it doesn't need to, since in the aggregate, it results in an efficient overall market. And sure beats the government telling us where and how to allocate resources. The problem comes when this pursuit of self-interest trumps a person's professional obligations and responsibilities.

In the financial industry, there are all sorts of explicit and implicit agreements when it comes to investing, managing, and protecting other people's money. These all have one thing in common—an obligation to operate ethically. When this obligation breaks down, as with incentives that encourage violations of these agreements, bad things happen. These violations include CEOs who get paid more even when their shareholders suffer; accounting firms and rating agencies that treat as "clients" the companies they're paid to evaluate; regulators who lower standards to increase the number of banks in their domain; politicians who use government money and guarantees to aid the short term and get more votes at the cost of the longer term; and individuals who lie or are allowed to do so on credit applications. Unfortunately, the few bad actors spoil it for the many good ones, and did so in such a way during the financial crisis that it severely damaged our banking sector and our economy and hurt our trust in the financial system.

That's why I think the work I do has meaning. If I can change the way that banks function, even a little, by removing some of the worst practices and highlighting the best, then I've accomplished something significant.

I have a cousin who graduated from West Point and later fought in Iraq. When he returned from his deployment, he spoke to my son's class, and one of the kids asked who or what his biggest enemy was. He reflected and then said, "Poverty." Economic development is a force for good in the world, and capitalism is the instrument by which that happens. But for it to work, it needs to be transparent. It needs people in charge who are acting as agents of something larger than their own, sometimes conflicting, self-interest.

■ ■ ■

Over the span of my career, I started out looking for money and found meaning. Almost two decades ago, I thought that achieving the Number would free me from worry. I did not yet have to withhold life support from my stepdad while sitting alone in a Pompano Beach, Florida, hospital on a sunny spring day. My mother had not yet died from a years-long battle with cancer. My wife had not yet suffered through the tragic death of her father after a botched surgery in a New Jersey hospital. I didn't yet know that eating breakfast with my kids on a Saturday morning would bring me such joy, especially when they ordered just one thing and actually ate it. To think that money would suffice in place of experiences like that or that it would take away the pain of loss—I just had no idea how narrow my goal was compared to what I would encounter in life.

Each step of the way, I worried about the consequences of a setback, peering only at a small isolated slice of existence, which often failed to relate to my future. For years, I failed to land an interview on Wall Street but gained strong experience at the Fed, had some fun, and met my wife. I worked for a harsh boss at UBS, but I learned the ropes. The deal makers almost kicked me out of Lehman, but this set me up to make the call of my career, when I went negative on the entire banking sector in 1999. I was fired from Credit Suisse but got out before the firm went through a rash of regulatory problems, and I found my redemption.

I still don't think I have all the answers. I don't go to work each day or even each year consciously thinking about the grand purpose I serve. Like most people, I simply think about doing a good job. I still have major professional goals. But, mostly, I think I've learned that the work is its own reward. The meaning of life? For me, it's getting up every morning, kissing my wife, hugging my kids, and heading off to work.

Acknowledgments

Thank you to my bank team, the workhorses—Chris Spahr, Rob Rutschow, Matt Fischer, Tom Hennessy, and Tom Shearer—who not only supported this book with analysis, insight, and review but do so every day with our research. CLSA has been a big supporter of my independence and this book, especially Jonathan Slone, Edmund Bradley, Jay Plourde, Grace Hung, and Simon Harris, all of whom continue the legacy of founder Gary Coull. Much appreciation to Mary Beth Kissane for encouraging the concept, Jeff Garigliano for helping me find my voice, and Laura Walsh and the others at Wiley for making this happen. Of course, there are my children, Lily, Sam, and Stella, and wife, Jackie, who helped with many late-night edits and may someday realize that I ask all the right questions.

About the Author

One of the top-ranked banking and finance analysts for the past twenty years, Mike Mayo has worked at Wall Street firms including UBS, Lehman Brothers, Credit Suisse, Prudential Securities, and Deutsche Bank, and is currently at Credit Agricole Securities, which provides services in the U.S. for CLSA, a global boutique brokerage firm. In 2008, *Fortune* named him one of "8 Who Saw the Crisis Coming." Mayo was the only analyst to testify during Senate Banking Committee hearings in 2002 on conflicts of interest on Wall Street. In 2010, he again testified as the first analyst following the roster of bank CEOs speaking before the Financial Crisis Inquiry Commission on the causes of the crisis.

Notes

Introduction

Fortune magazine: "8 Who Saw the Crisis Coming—and 8 Who Didn't," August 6, 2008. http://money.cnn.com/galleries/2008/fortune/0808/gallery .whosawitcoming.fortune/index.html.

Dick Parsons: Devin Leonard, "Dick Parsons, Captain Emergency," *Bloomberg Businessweek*, March 24, 2011. www.businessweek.com/magazine/content/ 11_14/b4222084044889.htm.

Putin: Maria Tsvetkova, "Putin Says U.S. Is 'Parasite' on Global Economy," Reuters, August 1, 2011. www.reuters.com/article/2011/08/01/us-russia-putin-usa-idUSTRE77052R20110801.

Chapter 1

Many of the stories about my stepdad come from his unpublished memoir. Details on the Vagabond restaurant are from a review in *Washington Jewish Week*, June 18, 1992.

Protests over Volcker's raising of interest rates: Gary H. Stern, "Interview with Paul A. Volcker," Federal Reserve Bank of Minneapolis (September 2009). www.minneapolisfed.org/publications_papers/pub_display.cfm?id= 4292.

Volcker's quote about financial innovation: "Paul Volcker: Think More Boldly," *Wall Street Journal*, December 14, 2009. http://online.wsj.com/article/ SB10001424052748704825504574586330960597134.html.

George Soros quote: Krishna Guha and Gillian Tett, "Man in the News: Paul Volcker," *Financial Times*, April 11, 2008. www.ft.com/intl/cms/s/0/ 47155caa-0796-11df-915f-00144feabdc0.html#axzz1WdCHvIrJ.

Lloyd Blankfein: John Arlidge, "I'm Doing 'God's Work': Meet Mr. Goldman Sachs," *Sunday Times* (London), November 8, 2009. www.timesonline.co.uk/ tol/news/world/us_and_americas/article6907681.ece.

S&L crisis: A good discussion on the causes of the crisis and lessons learned comes from L. William Seidman, who chaired the FDIC and later the Resolution Trust Corporation, the government agency that essentially nationalized problem S&Ls during the crisis. Seidman gave this background in a speech to some bankers in 1996, with the benefit of historical perspective: www.fdic .gov/bank/historical/history/vol2/panel3.pdf.

Bill Taylor: obituary in the *Independent*, August 29, 1992.

Bill Taylor quote about the quality of staffers at the Fed comes from a Q&A he did with the Federal Reserve Bank of Minneapolis in February 1990. In that same interview, when asked about the main lessons learned from the S&L debacle, Taylor gave a prophetic answer: "The whole thing offers many lessons, most of which have been taught before. Fast growth, unstable funding sources, human frailty and a lack of controls can severely damage an institution—but the big gamble that causes the most fatalities is in the area of asset quality. Making loans (or equity investments) that do not generate sufficient cash flow to service the debt and cover the risks involved is the greatest danger facing financial institutions, including banks." That's as true today as it was when he said it in 1990. www.minneapolisfed.org/publications_papers/pub_display.cfm?id=3791.

Details about the conference room where the Fed chairman and governors meet come from Roger Lowenstein, "The Education of Ben Bernanke," *New York Times Magazine*, January 20, 2008. Also the Fed's Web site: www.federalreserve .gov/boarddocs/meetings/brdroom.htm.

Ernie Patrikis's biography: From the Web site of White & Case (www.whitecase .com), where he now serves as a partner.

Head of the New York Fed and affair with the head of the Boston Fed: Peter Truell, "A Fed Official's Romance Raises Issue of Conflict," *New York Times*, April 9, 1997. www.nytimes.com/1997/04/09/business/a-fed-official- s-romance-raises-issue-of-conflict.html.

Wayne Angell's prediction on interest rates: Silvia Nasar, "Inquiry Finds No Evidence of Leak to Ex-Fed Governor," *New York Times*, June 16, 1994. www.nytimes.com/1994/06/16/business/inquiry-finds-no-evidence-of- leak-to-ex-fed-governor.html.

Chapter 2

"Wall Street" quote: www.imdb.com/title/tt0094291/quotes.

Tom Hanley's departure from First Boston: Beth Selby, "How Tom Hanley Got a Raise for His Old Colleagues," *Institutional Investor* (February 1991)

Tom Hanley: Saul Hansell, "Market Place: When Thomas Hanley Starts Spreading Bank Merger Rumors, Many Serious Investors Listen," *New York Times*, September 19, 1997.

Hanley's call on the Banker's Trust merger: Timothy O'Brien, "Egg on Face, but Analyst May Profit," *New York Times*, November 20, 1997. nytimes.com/1997/11/20/business/market-place-egg-on-face-but-analyst-may-profit.html?pagewanted=print&src=pm.

Hanley's SEC settlement: Floyd Norris, "Rumor Leads to Censures and Fines," *New York Times*, June 29, 2000. nytimes.com/2000/06/29/business/the-markets-market-place-rumor-leads-to-censures-and-fines.html?pagewanted=print&src=pm.

Keefe CEO's insider trading scandal: *Time*, Top 10 CEO Scandals, August 10, 2010. www.time.com/time/specials/packages/article/0,28804,2009445_2009447_2009457,00.html.

John McCoy wins Banker of the Year in 1992: www.americanbanker.com/boty/bankeroftheyeararchive.html.

Interstate banking law: The full name of the law is the Riegle–Neal Interstate Banking and Branching Efficiency Act, www.fdic.gov/regulations/laws/important/index.html.

Performance of bank stocks after my positive call in late 1994: David Rynecki, "The Price of Being Right," *Fortune*, February 5, 2001.

Chapter 3

Credit Suisse's involvement in the tech bubble after hiring Quattrone: "Ex–CSFB Banker Frank Quattrone Faces Criminal Charges," Bloomberg, April 23, 2003.

The Red Queen Effect: Lewis Carroll, *Through the Looking-Glass, and What Alice Found There* (New York: W. W. Norton & Company, 1871).

My negative call in 1999 and the subsequent backlash: David Rynecki, "The Price of Being Right," *Fortune*, February 5, 2001.

Bulletin board photo of me: Robert McGough, "Bearish Call on Banks Lands Analyst in Doghouse," *Wall Street Journal*, November 23, 1999.

Wall Street Journal story on potential bank takeovers: Stephen E. Frank, "Bank Stocks Could Hold Allure Again," *Wall Street Journal*, May 29, 1996.

Harvard woman going negative on banks: "Analyst Roundtable: Fourth Quarter a Tough Call; Deposit Growth Impresses," *American Banker*, November 9, 2001.

Infectious greed: "Testimony of Alan Greenspan: Federal Reserve Board's semi-annual monetary policy report to the Congress, before the Committee on Banking, Housing, and Urban Affairs, U.S. Senate," July 16, 2002. www .federalreserve.gov/boarddocs/hh/2002/july/testimony.htm.

Grubman sanctions: Bloomberg, April 23, 2003, Ibid.

Credit Suisse settlement over tech IPOs: Civil Action No. 03 Civ. 2946 (WHP), final settlement. www.sec.gov/litigation/litreleases/judg18110.pdf. The $200 million in total costs comes from analysis by my team.

Grubman: "Is Jack Grubman the Worst Analyst Ever?" *Money* magazine, April 25, 2002.

Grubman's e-mail and memo to Sandy Weill were released in a Frontline documentary about Wall Street: "The Wall Street Fix," first aired on May 9, 2003. www.pbs.org/wgbh/pages/frontline/shows/wallstreet/wcom/ 92memo.html.

Grubman's SEC settlement: "The Securities and Exchange Commission, New York Attorney General's Office, NASD, and the New York Stock Exchange Permanently Bar Jack Grubman and Require $15 Million Payment," April 28, 2003, http://www.sec.gov/news/press/2003-55.htm.

Merrill Lynch tech analyst with ties to Tyco: "NASD Fines and Suspends Phua Young, Former Merrill Lynch Research Analyst," FINRA, May 25, 2004. www.finra.org/Newsroom/NewsReleases/2004/P002827.

Anti-Blodgett: Landon Thomas Jr., "Super Geek Mike Mayo Says Sell Those Bank Stocks—and Do Your Homework," *New York Observer*, November 26, 2001.

Dennis Kozlowski: Peter Lattman, "Dennis Kozlowski: Prisoner 05A4820," *Wall Street Journal* law blog, March 26, 2007.

Spitzer settlement: "Ten of Nation's Top Investment Firms Settle Enforcement Actions Involving Conflicts of Interest Between Research and Investment Banking," SEC release, April 28, 2003. www.sec.gov/news/press/2003-54.htm.

My testimony: "Accounting and Investor Protection Issues Raised by Enron and Other Public Companies," U.S. Senate Banking Committee hearing, March 19, 2002. banking.senate.gov/02_03hrg/031902/mayo.htm.

Chapter 4

Jamie Dimon: David Wighton, "JPMorgan Chief in Spat with Analyst Over Stock Picks," *Financial Times*, February 9, 2006. www.ft.com/intl/cms/ s/0/8b9e68b8-98f9-11da-aa99-0000779e2340.html#axzz1Wjd8dfax. Also, "JPMorgan CEO's Joke Upsets Analyst," Dow Jones Newswires, February 10, 2006.

Chapter 5

Demise of Prudential: Suzanne Craig, "Prudential's Last Research Call: 'Bye,' " *Wall Street Journal*, June 7, 2007.

Fortune magazine: "8 Who Saw the Crisis Coming—and 8 Who Didn't," August 6, 2008. http://money.cnn.com/galleries/2008/fortune/0808/gallery .whosawitcoming.fortune/index.html.

Mortgage refinancing statistics: "Characteristics and Performance of Nonprime Mortgages," GAO Report No. GAO-09-848R, July 28, 2009; cited in "Wall Street and the Financial Crisis: Anatomy of a Financial Collapse," U.S. Senate Permanent Subcommittee on Investigations, April 13, 2011, p. 21. www.ft.com/intl/cms/fc7d55c8-661a-11e0-9d40-00144feab49a.pdf.

Jamie Dimon quote about housing prices: Michael Hiltzik, "A Damning Post-Mortem of the Financial Meltdown," *Los Angeles Times*, February 6, 2011. articles.latimes.com/2011/feb/06/business/la-fi-hiltzik-20110206.

Bear Stearns hedge funds: Peter Stiff, "Bear Stearns: Timeline to Disaster," *Times* (London), March 14, 2008.

Chuck Prince management restructuring in October 2007: Robin Sidel and David Enrich, "Citigroup CEO Shakes Up Ranks," *Wall Street Journal*, October 12, 2007. http://online.wsj.com/article/SB119215044797956833 .html?mod=hps_us_whats_news.

Prince's "We're still dancing" quote: Michiyo Nakamoto and David Wighton, "Citigroup Chief Stays Bullish on Buy-outs," *Financial Times*, July 9, 2007.

Prince's subsequent testimony: Cyrus Sanati, "Prince Finally Explains His Dancing Comment," *New York Times* Dealbook, April 8, 2010.

Rubin's defense of Prince: Barrie McKenna, "Rubin Has Credentials, but Can He Save Citi?" *Globe and Mail*, November 6, 2007.

Rubin's background: Eric Dash and Sewell Chan, "Panel Criticized Oversight of Citi by 2 Executives," *New York Times*, April 8, 2010. Also, *New York Times* background profile of Robert E. Rubin, as part of the paper's *Times* Topics coverage, August 12, 2010. http://topics.nytimes.com/top/reference/ timestopics/people/r/robert_e_rubin/index.html?inline=nyt-per.

My appearance on CNBC to talk about downgrading Citi: "Call of the Day," CNBC, October 12, 2007, 1:12 P.M.; clip at www.stockmaven.com/video/ Mayo101207ET112PM.htm.

Citi's third-quarter earnings announcement transcript: SeekingAlpha.com, posted October 15, 2007. http://seekingalpha.com/article/49937-citigroup-q3-2007-earnings-call-transcript.

My question during Citi's earnings call: "The Chuck Prince-Mike Mayo Food Fight," *Wall Street Journal* Deal Journal blog, October 15, 2007. http://blogs .wsj.com/deals/2007/10/15/the-chuck-prince-michael-mayo-food-fight/.

Chuck Prince's salary: Citigroup's proxy statement, Schedule 14A, p. 39, filed with the SEC on March 14, 2006. edgar.brand.edgar-online.com/displayfilinginfo .aspx?FilingID=4275399-1155-395817&type=sect&TabIndex=2&companyid= 12025&ppu=%252fdefault.aspx%253fcompanyid%253d12025%2526amp% 253bformtypeId%253d148.

Merrill Lynch's awful third quarter in 2007: Stephen Bernard, "Merrill Lynch Will Post 3Q Loss after $5 Billion in Write-Downs," *USA Today*, October 5, 2007.

Investment banks buying mortgage originators: Alistair Barr, "Lehman Shuts Sub-Prime Lending Unit, Eliminating 1,200 Jobs," *Marketwatch*, August 22, 2007.

$400 billion estimate: "Analysts See Subprime Losses Reaching $400 Billion," CNBC, November 12, 2007. www.cnbc.com/id/21753805/Analysts_See_ Subprime_Losses_Reaching_400_Billion.

Paulson's $3.7 billion year in 2007: "Who Is John Paulson?" *New York Times*, April 16, 2010. Also, John Paulson: Daniel Gross interview with Gregory Zuckerman, "The Greatest Trade Ever," *Newsweek*, November 9, 2009.

Deutsche Bank's proprietary positions during the crisis: "Wall Street and the Financial Crisis: Anatomy of a Financial Collapse," Ibid, p. 10.

Chapter 6

Lehman downgrade: Andrew Ross Sorkin, *Too Big to Fail* (New York: Viking, 2009). Also, David Gaffen, "Mega-Analyst Box Score: Lehman Brothers," *Wall Street Journal* Market Beat blog, September 11, 2008. blogs.wsj.com/ marketbeat/2008/09/11/mega-analyst-box-score-lehman-brothers/.

History of mortgages during the Great Depression: "Mortgage Innovation and Consumer Choice," Federal Reserve Bank of San Francisco Economic Letter, November 2006-38. www.frbsf.org/publications/economics/letter/ 2006/el2006-38.html. Thanks to Bart Dzivi, a securities lawyer and special counsel for the Financial Crisis Inquiry Commission, for pointing this out to me.

Darrel Dochow: Binyamin Appelbaum and Ellen Nakashima, "Regulator Let IndyMac Falsify Report," *Washington Post*, December 23, 2008. www.washingtonpost .com/wp-dyn/content/article/2008/12/22/AR2008122201301_pf.html.

More on Dochow: Pallavi Gogoi, "Bank Regulator Dochow Out over Backdating at IndyMac," *USA Today*, December 22, 2008.

On Countrywide's change of regulators and the OTS culture during the crisis: Binyamin Appelbaum and Ellen Nakashima, "Banking Regulator Played Advocate over Enforcer," *Washington Post*, November 23, 2008.

Chapter 7

February 2008 letter to Vikram Pandit: Jonathan Weil, "What Vikram Pandit Knew, and When He Knew It," Bloomberg, February 23, 2011. www .bloomberg.com/news/2011-02-24/what-vikram-pandit-knew-and-when-he-knew-it-commentary-by-jonathan-weil.html.

"Citigroup Under Fire over Disclosure": Francesco Guerrera, *Financial Times*, March 1, 2011.

Outmanned regulators: Author interview with Bart Dzivi, former counsel for the Senate Banking Committee; May 10, 2011.

Sarbanes-Oxley: sox-online.com/whatis.html. Section 302 of the law requires that CEOs sign off on financials. Section 404 outlines the specific review of internal controls. The law is fairly clear that banks can be in violation of it even if they haven't experienced significant problems due to insufficient controls. It's akin to the police citing you for reckless driving even if you didn't hit anyone.

Company giving back $1 for every $3 it earned: Susanne Craig, "Analyst's Street-Level View of Citi," *New York Times* Dealbook, October 4, 2010.

Citi's multiple near failures, particularly recently: Paul Krugman and Robin Wells, "The Busts Keep Getting Bigger: Why?" *The New York Review of Books*, July 14, 2011. www.nybooks.com/articles/archives/2011/jul/14/busts-keep-getting-bigger-why/?pagination=false.

Cuban sugar crisis and other early history of National City: Harold van B. Cleveland and Thomas F. Huertas, *Citibank: 1812–1970* (Cambridge, MA: Harvard University Press, 1885). This book is extremely thorough but not impartial, as both authors were executives at Citibank, and it was intended as an in-house history of the bank.

Storefront locations: Gretchen Morgenson, "Can Citi Carry Its Own Weight?" *New York Times*, October 31, 2009.

Carter Glass quote about Charles Mitchell: "Damnation of Mitchell," *Time*, March 6, 1933. www.time.com/time/magazine/article/0,9171,745272,00.html.

Pecora Commission: Ibid.

State bank limits during Mitchell's testimony: Nicholas Rugoff, "The Hellhound of Wall Street: An Interview with Michael Perino," *The Politic*, March 1, 2011; Perino is the author of a recent biography of Ferdinand Pecora.

Latin American debt: Phillip Zweig, *Wriston: Walter Wriston, Citibank, and the Rise and Fall of American Financial Supremacy* (New York: Crown Business, 1996).

Wriston quote about countries not going broke, from his op-ed: "Banking Against Disaster," *The New York Times*, September 14, 1982, from the Wriston archives at Tufts. http://hdl.handle.net/10427/57558.

Weill, more than a hundred acquisitions: "Sandy Weill: King of the High C," *Economist*, March 27, 2003.

Travelers spun off in 2002: Citigroup press release, "Citigroup Announces Completion of Its Spin-off of Travelers Property Casualty," August 20, 2002. http://web.archive.org/web/20070930160819; http://www.citigroup.com/citigroup/press/2002/020820a.htm.

Enron's dying days: Jeff Madrick, *The Age of Greed: The Triumph of Finance and the Decline of America, 1970 to the Present* (New York: Knopf, 2011), p. 339. Madrick's book is about changes to the entire financial system over the past four decades, but Citigroup appears more than any other company.

Japan private bank debacle: Todd Zaun, "Japan Shuts Unit of Citibank, Citing Violations," *New York Times*, September 18, 2008.

European bond scandal: Paivi Munter, "Citigroup Bond Trading Memor Revealed," *Financial Times*, January 31, 2005.

Internal controls were remiss: Julia Kollewe, "Citigroup Pays $13.9 Million to Settle with FSA over 'Dr. Evil' Bond Strategy," *Independent*, June 29, 2005.

Understated $40 billion in subprime exposure: William McQuillen "Citigroup $75 Million SEC Settlement Approved," Bloomberg, September 24, 2010.

Citigroup's defense: Ibid.

Terms of Citi's bailout: Special Inspector General for the Troubled Asset Relief Program (SIGTARP), "Extraordinary Financial Assistance Provided to Citigroup, Inc.," January 13, 2011, p. 25. www.sigtarp.gov/reports/audit/2011/Extraordinary%20Financial%20Assistance%20Provided%20to%20Citigroup,%20Inc.pdf.

"strikingly ad hoc": Ibid., p. 42.

Clear moral hazard: Ibid., p. 43.

December 2005 OCC letter: Bradley Keoun and Donal Griffin, "Citigroup Ignored 2005 Bond Warning After Shedding 'Handcuffs,'" *Bloomberg Businessweek*, January 28, 2011.

May 2008 letter from the New York Fed: SIGTARP report, p. 23.

"$4 to $5 billion a quarter": "The Financial Crisis Inquiry Report: Final Report of the National Commission on the Causes of the Financial and Economic Crisis in the United States," January 2011, p. 335. www.gpoaccess.gov/fcic/fcic.pdf.

Chapter 8

Vikram Pandit quote: conference call to discuss second-quarter 2010 earnings with analysts, 2010; Transcript from FactSet CallStreet, July 16, 2010.

Harvard case study: Suraj Srinivasan and Amy Kaser, "Mike Mayo Takes on Citigroup." September 2011. Harvard Business School Case 9-112-025.

"cheap sangria": "Financial Crisis Inquiry Report," Ibid, p. 6.

"Citi's position defies imagination and logic": Francesco Guerrera and Jean Eaglesham, "Citi Under Fire over Deferred Tax Assets," *Financial Times*, September 6, 2010.

Coverage of the 2010 standoff: Charlie Gasparino, "Analyst: Citigroup Is Cooking the books," FoxBusiness.com, August 25, 2010. Also, David Weidner, "At Citigroup the Hits—and Misses—Keep on Coming," *Wall Street Journal*, September 2, 2010. Mark DeCambre, "No Holding Mayo Back in His Feud with Citi," *New York Post*, August 31, 2010. Charlie Gasparino, "Do Banks Still Play Us for Fools?" *Daily Beast*, September 13, 2010. Susanne Craig, "After a Long Wait, a Critic of Citigroup Wins a Meeting with Top Executives," *New York Times*, September 26, 2010.

Citi's postmeeting attempt to undercut my report: Susanne Craig, "Investment Banking Citi Counters Critic; Stock Surges," *New York Times* Dealbook, October 1, 2010.

Vikram Pandit pay package: Justin Baer, "Full Steam Ahead for Citi Skipper Pandit," *Financial Times*, May 22, 2011. Also, Randall Smith, "Citi CEO Gets a Big Retention Deal—Package Aims to keep Pandit at the Helm Through 2015; His Pay Draws Fire from Critics," *Wall Street Journal*, May 18, 2011.

Dick Parsons on CNBC to defend Pandit's compensation: "Key to the Citi with Dick Parsons," May 19, 2011. video.cnbc.com/gallery/?video=3000022379.

Old Lane Partners: David Gaffen, "A (Brief) History of Old Lane Partners," WallStreetJournal.com Marketbeat, June 12, 2008. http://blogs.wsj.com/ marketbeat/2008/06/12/a-brief-history-of-old-lane-partners/. Gaffen called the fund "one of the quickest flame-outs since Mark Fidrych, a few of the mid-80s managers of the New York Yankees, and Erin Callan's tenure as CFO of Lehman Brothers."

Sheila Bair, "…we are going to be back in here writing checks": SIGTARP report, p. 23.

Chapter 9

Transfer of securities in 2009: Jennifer Hughes, "Banks' Toxic Accounting," *Financial Times*, April 19, 2011.

Lehman's repo 105 deals: Michael de la Merced and Andrew Ross Sorkin, "Report Details How Lehman Hid Its Woes as It Collapsed," *New York Times*, March 11, 2003. www.nytimes.com/2010/03/12/business/12lehman.html?dbk.

Wilmington Trust: David Mildenberg and Zachary R. Mider, "Wilmington Trust's Half-Price Sale to MT Ends DuPont Legacy," *Bloomberg Businessweek*,

November 2, 2011. www.businessweek.com/news/2010-11-02/wilmington-trust-s-half-price-sale-to-m-t-ends-du-pont-legacy.html.

Bank of America audit fees: Company proxy statement, Schedule 14A, p. 51, filed with the SEC on May 11, 2011, p. 51. google.brand.edgar-online .com/displayfilinginfo.aspx?FilingID=7828109-1255-378593&type=sect& TabIndex=2&companyid=15519&ppu=%252fdefault.aspx%253fcompanyid% 253d15519%2526amp%253bformtypeId%253d148.

PCAOB research: James R. Doty, "Rethinking the Relevance, Credibility and Transparency of Audits," speech given at the SEC and Financial Reporting Institute 30th Annual Conference, June 2, 2011, Pasadena, California. http:// pcaobus.org/News/Speech/Pages/06022011_DotyKeynoteAddress.aspx.

Brandeis quote about sunshine: Louis Brandeis, "Other People's Money," *Harper's*, December 20, 1913.

Warren Buffett quote: Fox Business News interview, January 20, 2010. http:// wallstreetpit.com/14820-warren-buffett-if-a-bank-fails-the-ceo-and-his-wife-should-forfeit-their-net-worth.

McKinsey survey: "Governance Since the Economic Crisis," *McKinsey Quarterly* (July 2011). www.mckinseyquarterly.com/Governance_since_the_economic_ crisis_McKinsey_Global_Survey_results_2814.

Proportion of sell ratings on Wall Street remains only 5 percent: "Only 5.1% of Analyst Ratings Say to Sell," *San Francisco Chronicle*, May 22, 2011, citing Bloomberg data. www.sfgate.com/cgi-bin/article.cgi?f=/c/a/2011/05/21/ BUT51JIV47.DTL.

Study about screening questions during earnings calls: "NIRI Survey Reveals the Latest Earnings Call Practices," National Investor Relations Institute, April 4, 2011.

BofA, loss projections before taxes or after: Fourth-quarter 2010 earnings call, January 21, 2011. Transcript from FactSet CallStreet.

KeyCorp CEO saying my question was offensive: Maria Woehr, "Analyst Questions KeyCorp Loan Moves," *The Street*, March 12, 2011. www.thestreet .com/story/11041030/1/analyst-questions-keycorp-loan-moves.html.

Capital One's limited disclosure: Company press release, July 13, 2011; http:// phx.corporate-ir.net/External.File?item+UGFyZW50SUQ9Otk5ODF8Q2 hpbGRJRD0tMXxUeXBlPTM=&t=1.

Goldman Sachs earnings release: Company press release, January 19, 2011. http:// www2.goldmansachs.com/our-firm/press/press-releases/current/2011-01-19-q4-results.html.

Finance industry spent $2.7 billion on lobbying efforts: FCIC report, p. xviii.

Direct correlation between lobbying by lenders and a decrease in regulation: Deniz Igan, Prachi Mishra, and Thierry Tressel, "A Fistful of Dollars: Lobbying and the Financial Crisis," NBER Working Paper No. 17076, May 2011.

Head of Nigerian Central Bank quotes: "An Assessment of Current Development in the Nigerian Economy and the Central Bank of Nigeria (CBN) Policy Action," speech by Sanusi Lamido Aminu Sanusi, Governor of the CBN, at a press conference in Abuja, July 7, 2009. www.bis.org/review/r090717e.pdf. Also Ruona Agbroko, "Where is Cecilia Ibru? (The Sacked Chief Executive of Oceanic Bank," Free Republic, August 26, 2009. www.freerepublic.com/focus/f-news/2324722/posts.

Alan Greenspan quote about market regulation: Alan Greenspan, "Remarks," speech on government regulation and derivative contracts at the Financial Markets Conference of the Atlanta Fed, Coral Gables, Florida, February 21, 1997. http://www.federalreserve.gov/boarddocs/speeches/1997/19970221.htm.

Greenspan's subsequent recanting: Edmund L. Andrews, "Greenspan Concedes Error on Regulation," *New York Times*, October 23, 2008.

Chapter 10

Analyst fired over Trump Taj Mahal comments: Richard Burke, "Fired Janney Securities Analyst Sues Trump," *Philadelphia Inquirer*, July 11, 1990.

Index